T·O·W·N·A·N·D·C·I·T·Y·G·U·I·D·E·S

AA

CAMBRIDGE

T·O·W·N·A·N·D·C·I·T·Y·G·U·I·D·E·S

The all-in-one guide to what goes on in and around the city

*Tourist information,
maps, walks, drives,
eating out, where to stay*

Produced by the Publishing Division of the Automobile Association

Front cover: King's College Chapel and the Backs

Editor: Rebecca Snelling
Copy Editor: Karin Fancett
Art Editor: Peter Davies
Design Assistant: John Breeze
Original Photography: Malc Birkitt
Picture Researcher: Wyn Voysey
Editorial Contributors: Sue Bryan (City Walks), Mac Dowdy (A Selection of Architecture), Arthur Harradine (The Fens, The City and its History, The University, King's College Chapel), Diana & Lionel Munby (City Centre: Places to Visit, Open Spaces), Honour Ridout (Out of City: Places to Visit, Famous Students)

Directory compiled by Karin Fancett

Day Drives prepared by the Home Routes Research and Development Unit of the Automobile Association

Maps and plans produced by the Cartographic Department of the Automobile Association. Atlas based on the Ordnance Survey maps, reproduced with the permission of the controller of Her Majesty's Stationery Office. Crown copyright reserved.

Filmset by Vantage Photosetting Co Ltd, Eastleigh and London, England

Printed and bound by Graficromo SA, Spain

The contents of this publication are believed correct at the time of printing. Nevertheless, the Publishers cannot accept responsibility for errors or omissions, or for changes in details given

© The Automobile Association 1988

Published by the Publishing Division of the Automobile Association

Produced and distributed in the United Kingdom by the Publishing Division of the Automobile Association, Fanum House, Basingstoke, Hampshire, RG21 2EA

ISBN 0 86145 651 3
AA Reference 50746

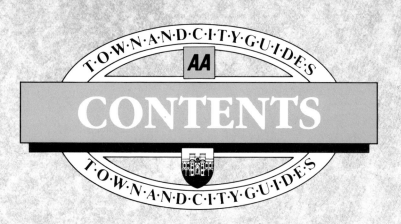

CONTENTS

Introduction

CLASSIC CAMBRIDGE
The Backs behind King's College

As part of the longstanding rivalry between the ancient university towns of Oxford and Cambridge, students at the former may refer disparagingly to Cambridge as a 'small market town in the Fens'. This was indeed a true description during Roman, Saxon, Danish and Norman times. However, the arrival of a group of scholars, fleeing from riots in Oxford in the early 13th century, was the start of the transformation of Cambridge into a city best known for, and largely dominated by, its University and colleges.

As the numbers of students increased, and rich benefactors put money into the founding of colleges, some magnificent buildings were designed and constructed, and it is to these that visitors to Cambridge tend to make a beeline. King's College Chapel is, of course, the most famous, but many other buildings, grand or intimate, ancient or modern, are well worth visiting and are described in more detail later in this book, both in the city gazetteer and in the feature article on the architecture of Cambridge.

Many of the buildings of Cambridge indisputably gain much from their setting against the city's numerous open spaces. Close to the city centre are the fairly urban Parker's and Christ's 'Pieces', whilst the River Cam, as it curves through the city, is bordered for most of its length by 'Greens' and 'Commons' and, of course, 'The Backs'.

The river provides one of the most relaxing ways to see some of the sights of Cambridge, providing you can persuade someone else to do the hard work of propelling your punt and avoiding the bridges and banks! The city centre itself is best explored on foot; alternatively try Cambridge's other popular mode of transport—the bicycle.

However you travel, try to find time to see some of the city's many cultural treasures. Cambridge has museums catering for a wide range of interests, from the fine arts at the Fitzwilliam, to the history of science at the Whipple. Those interested in literature will no doubt want to visit libraries such as that of Pepys at Magdalene, as well as the colleges of great poets and writers, including Milton, Byron and Wordsworth. Meanwhile, geologists, zoologists, anthropologists or archaeologists will find much to interest them in the University's departmental museums as well as in the city's links with great scientists like Darwin. American visitors will almost certainly wish to see the memorial to Godfrey Washington in Little St Mary's Church, and Emmanuel, the college of so many of the early emigrants to New England.

In attempting to describe the character

of Cambridge, it must not be forgotten that the city is still a market town and also the county town of Cambridgeshire. To serve its own population of just over 100,000 people, together with many others from the surrounding countryside, it provides a range of facilities. Nearly all the major chain and department stores can be found in its city centre and the new Grafton Centre, together with many specialist shops, including bookshops—as might be expected in a university town. Cultural pursuits and sports are also well catered for, whether you wish to participate or spectate, perhaps trying your hand at talent-spotting as you watch the young actors or comedians on stage at the Footlights Revue or cricketers playing at Fenner's, the University ground.

With this wealth of things to do in the city itself it may be difficult to drag yourself away to visit the surrounding towns, villages and countryside. But then you would miss the wide open views across the fenland and the industrial and rural museums that depict aspects of the region's fascinating history as the Fens were drained and converted to rich agricultural land. You would also miss many grand country houses, churches and abbeys, each of which has its own history to tell, from the wool churches of Lavenham and Long Melford in the

A COUNTY TOWN
The hustle and bustle of Market Place

south-east of the region to the Elizabethan mansion of Burghley in the north-west, with many others in between.

The wide variety of attractions both within and around Cambridge mean that it is a city that can be enjoyed in all seasons. Whatever time of year you choose, do come to sample some of the delights of this city which is still 'a market town in the Fens' but also much, much more.

About This Book

Cambridge City Guide,
designed to be the complete guide for tourist or resident,
contains the following sections.

Features
Written by local experts, these introductory articles cover
subjects of special importance in the city—from its history and
beautiful buildings to the desolate charm of the surrounding
fenland and the impact of the University and its students over
the centuries.

City Centre: Places to Visit
Here places of interest, listed alphabetically, are described in
detail. Each entry includes the street name, so it can easily be
located on the street plan on page 102. For opening times and
practical information refer to the Directory.

City Walks
Six walks, with step-by-step route directions, have been
carefully planned to take in the best of the city. A clear, easy-to-
follow map accompanies each walk. The chief places of interest
along the way are described in the text, and these are keyed to
the maps by numbers.

Out of City: Places to Visit
An alphabetical selection of the most attractive and interesting
towns, villages and places to visit in the surrounding area. All
are within an hour or so's drive. For opening times etc refer to
the relevant section of the Directory. Each entry has a grid
reference, so can be located on the maps on pages 96—99.

Day Drives
Two routes for exploring the countryside around the city,
including detailed route directions, a map and places of
interest.

District Maps
Four pages of mapping at a scale of 4 miles to the inch,
covering the area around the city, extending approximately 35
miles from the city centre.

Throughroute Map
This shows the motorways and main roads in and out of the
city.

City Plan
A large-scale map of the city centre, with a street index and
places of interest clearly marked.

Directory
Twelve pages packed with useful information grouped into
sections (see page 105). All you need to know about where to
eat and stay, recreation, shops, sports and services, plus useful
addresses and opening times for all the places of interest
described in the book.

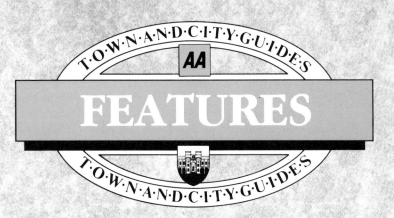

FEATURES

Coat of arms belonging to Downing College. William
Wilkins, after winning a competition to design the buildings,
selected a neo-Grecian style

The Cambridge Year

ON THE RIVER
Since the 1820s, the 'Bumps' (below) with characters like 'the Coach' (above) have been part of the Cambridge scene

T he residents of Cambridge often reckon to be able to tell the time of year by the concentration of student-propelled bicycles on King's Parade and the nationality of visiting tourists. Inevitably the 'student' events are concentrated in the six or seven months of term-time, but Cambridge has something happening all year round, with most events open to students, townspeople and visitors alike. The listing below is by month, but some dates vary a little from year to year, so exact timing should be checked with the Tourist Information Centre.

JANUARY
Linking the old year and the new is the annual Christmas Pantomime at the Arts Theatre. Lent Term begins around the middle of the month.

FEBRUARY
This is the month for the first intercollege rowing races, or 'Lents'. About 15 boats at a time line up, each a boat-length-and-a-half behind the next. The idea is to catch up with, or 'bump', the boat in front and in so doing take their place in the league. Also held in February or early March is Rag Week—a mid-term chance for students to let their hair down by performing stunts and organising events for charity.

MARCH
No sooner do the students seem to have arrived back, than it is vacation time again! By going away, however, they may well miss some of the magnificent displays of daffodils and crocuses to be seen on the Backs at this time of year.

APRIL
Easter usually heralds the start of the main tourist season in Cambridge. The punts are taken out of winter storage, and the tourist guides brush up on their dates and facts. On Midsummer Common the Fun Fair arrives for the first of its several visits during the year, and soon after Easter the students are back again for the new term.

"A Bump", Cambridge May Races.

Punting along the Backs is an ideal way to see many of the sights of Cambridge and is especially popular on warm summer afternoons

MAY

The Easter Term means exams for most students, so tours around the colleges are somewhat limited to provide peace and quiet for study. However, there is still plenty going on, with the Cambridge Rowing Regatta mid month and singing by St John's College Choir from the chapel tower on Ascension Day. The latter is a comparatively recent custom, introduced in 1904 by Dr Rootham, the college organist and choir master.

JUNE

Despite its name, 'May Week' occurs in early June, once the exams are over. It can be a social extravaganza (for those who have the money and the time!) with May Balls, plays in the college gardens, concerts and, of course, the traditional punting to Grantchester for breakfast. As well as watching elegant and sometimes not so elegant punting, riverside spectators can also listen to the singing of madrigals on the river from the Backs, or cheer on the teams in the 'May Bumps'. Like the 'Lents' earlier in the year, these are held on the stretch of the River Cam between Bait's Bite Lock, Milton, and Stourbridge Common.

Concurrent with 'May Week' and running for a fortnight, is the annual Footlights Revue at the Arts Theatre which has provided a debut for many of those well known in the entertainment world today.

At the end of the month, Midsummer

Fair is held on the common of this name. Formerly called the Pot Fair, because of the quantities of china sold there, this fair traces its origins back to the 13th century. Also at the end of the month, on the last or penultimate Friday and Saturday, the General Admission to Degrees (or Degree Ceremony) is held.

JULY

In mid July the city, as opposed to the University, holds its own festival, the Cambridge Festival. This starts with a carnival fair followed by fireworks on Parker's Piece, and during the two weeks of the Festival there are classical and popular music concerts, many theatrical events (including street theatre), films, international folk dancing displays, a marathon and the city 'Bumps'.

On the last weekend of the Festival, sometimes in early August, the Cambridge Folk Festival is held. This popular event attracts big names from the folk world as well as many excellent local performers. The major concerts take place in the open-air parkland setting of Cherry Hinton Hall, though there are large marquees for wet-weather use and for the numerous smaller events.

AUGUST

August is a fairly quiet month for organised events in Cambridge with many residents as well as students being away on holiday. At the end of the month, on August Bank Holiday, the Leisure Fair is held. This gives local clubs and societies a chance to publicise themselves and attract new members for the coming year.

SEPTEMBER

At the beginning of September, or sometimes in late August, the Cambridge Fun Run is held to raise money for charities as well as to provide exercise for the participants. Another September event is the Autumn Regatta which is held around the middle of the month.

OCTOBER

October, like April, is a time of changing populations. New students, or 'Freshers', as well as those returning for another year arrive for the Michaelmas Term, while the numbers of tourists dwindle and the punts are put away.

NOVEMBER

On Midsummer Common the Fun Fair arrives during the first week of November ready for Bonfire Night. This is celebrated on the common with a grand bonfire and firework display. Later on in the month, the Christmas lights go up in the city centre.

DECEMBER

Michaelmas Term ends, but King's College and its Choir School continue their preparation for the Festival of Nine Lessons and Carols to be held on Christmas Eve. Admission is free, but long queues form for this event which brings the Cambridge year to a close.

MADRIGALS AFLOAT
Punt-borne singers perform for the crowds gathered on the lawns in front of King's College Chapel

SUMMER CEREMONY
Midsummer Fair—or the Pot Fair—as it was depicted in 1777 (above), and as seen from the air today (far left). Now, as in the past, the fair is proclaimed open by the Mayor at noon on the first day

The Fens

The word 'Fen' may suggest an image of a cold, damp, foggy, flat and waterlogged area without a single redeeming feature. While this is undoubtedly one side of the picture, the fenlands nevertheless have a very special charm of their own. There are few places in England where an uninterrupted 180-degree view can be obtained, and the sight of large clouds sailing across a vast expanse of blue above the Fens is an unforgettable experience. Indeed, Rupert Brooke was so impressed that, in his poem *The Old Vicarage, Grantchester,* he wrote:

> . . . *I only know that you may lie*
> *Day long and watch the Cambridge sky.*

WIDE SKIES
A fenland view,
near Upware

The rivers and drainage channels criss-crossing the Fens are ideal for a tranquil boating holiday

THE PREHISTORY OF THE FENS

Until 10,000 years ago Great Britain was part of the continental mainland of Europe whose major river was the Rhine. The river flowed through land now submerged beneath the North Sea into the ocean south-west of Norway. In turn, the rivers Ouse, Nene and Welland drained large areas of what is now eastern England and emptied their waters into the Rhine.

Some 8,000 years BC the last Ice Age ended and rising temperatures meant that huge quantities of melted ice poured into the world's oceans. This led to the raising of the sea-level, and the consequent inundation of vast areas of land. As a result of the flooding, an area of some 1,300 square miles stretching from Cambridge in the south to Lincoln, and from King's Lynn in the east to Peterborough, was partly submerged. Cycles of flooding and drying out followed, leading to the formation of the fenland of today.

For centuries at a time the fenland would be flooded, but then the area would become drier and support pine and birch trees, shrubs, reeds and grasses. Then, once again the sea would overflow and the trees and shrubs would die and rot away. It was this decaying vegetation which laid down the beds of peat, often in excess of 60 ft deep, which provide such rich agricultural land today.

THE ROMANS

When the Romans came to Britain in the 1st century AD their engineers attempted to reclaim parts of the flooded fenland by straightening and deepening rivers and waterways and raising river banks to allow more water to be carried to the sea. The Romans were successful in recovering a few thousand acres of pasture-land, but following the withdrawal of the Legions in the 5th century AD, the native Britons allowed the waterways to silt up and the river banks to collapse, and once more the land returned to bog.

RELIGIOUS ISOLATION

For the next 500 years the fenland was practically a separate country from the rest of Britain, shunned by 'right thinking people'. This inhospitable land became a haven for religious zealots such as St Guthlac who arrived in the 7th century to set up an oratory. At about the same time St Etheldreda founded the religious house which later became Ely Cathedral. Many other religious houses sprang up in the Fens, including those at Peterborough and Thorney. These played their part in fen drainage as each reclaimed from the waters as much land as possible so that the monastery's estates could be extended.

St Guthlac, in his writings, describes his struggles with 'fearsome giants, with twisted faces and necks: wild staring eyes, foul breath and fire in their throats'. Today this seems a wild exaggeration—but is it? The wet, unhealthy surroundings of the fenland led to frequent occurrences of malaria (or ague) as well as rheumatic and respiratory disorders. There is an old fenland saying:

> *Poppy tea and opium pills*
> *Is the cure for fenland ills*

Did Guthlac seek to ease his miseries with the local medicines? If so, perhaps he did 'see' the giants he wrote of.

THE NORMANS

With the Norman invasion of England in 1066 came further attempts at draining the Fens. The drainage was undertaken partly because the Normans did not like to see such large areas of land lying idle when they could be used for grazing and cultivation. They were also keen to defeat Hereward the Wake, a local Saxon leader, who had refused to accept Norman rule and with a band of like-minded supporters had withdrawn to Ely. At that time Ely was simply a large island standing slightly higher than the surrounding marsh, and it could only be approached by people who knew their way across the waters. The Prior of Ely gave reluctant shelter to Hereward's knights, and from the fastness of Ely they raided the surrounding countryside.

William the Conqueror was not a man to accept such opposition, and by bargaining with the monks of Ely he was able to land troops on the island and defeat the insurgents. In 1081 he sent 86-year-old Prior Simeon to plan and build a new cathedral at Ely. Fortunately Simeon lived to be 100 and saw both the north and south transepts take shape.

The Normans dredged and widened rivers and rebuilt river banks, adding several thousand acres of useful land to the cathedral estates. All labour was manual, of course, and the silting up of the channels was a continuing problem; rivers changed their course, rivers 'disappeared' completely, and periodic 'drownings' often changed the face of the countryside beyond all recognition.

DRAINAGE STRUGGLES

Ever since Roman times man has had a constant battle to keep open the fenland drainage channels. Men would pass the mud from shovel to shovel up the bank; the steam dredger, photographed in about 1893, used revolving buckets and a conveyor belt to achieve the same end

THE ADVENTURERS AND THE UNDERTAKERS

A serious attempt at draining the Fens was started in the 1620s and 1630s when Charles I, under pressure from local

WICKEN WINDMILL
At one time allowed to become derelict, the windmill at Wicken Fen has now been restored and provides a striking landmark on this nature reserve

FENLAND LIFE
An old fenland couple with their fishing nets and traps photographed in the 1870s

landowners, took a long and serious look at the problem. Around this time also, two types of entrepreneurs, the 'Adventurers' and the 'Undertakers', came on the scene. The former were men willing to risk money in schemes for drainage in return for a percentage of the land recovered. The latter were the contractors who actually carried out the work.

The most famous of the Adventurers was the 4th Duke of Bedford, and it was he who, in 1630, employed the Dutch engineer Cornelius Vermuyden to construct an artificial river some 20 miles long, terminating in a sluice at Denver which prevented sea water flowing up the channel and causing flooding. This proved successful to a limited extent and in 1653 a new channel was cut running parallel to the Duke's channel and some half a mile away. These two rivers, the Old Bedford and the New Bedford, with their straight courses are an unmistakable feature on any map of the Fens.

The more successful the Adventurers were in reclaiming land, the more problems they created, for as the water level dropped the spongy peat dried out and the level of the land sunk, until thousands of acres lay well below the rivers and natural gravitational drainage was impossible. Again Dutch ideas were imported and hundreds of windmills were constructed. In the 19th century these began to be replaced by steam engines (the

first was installed by John Rennie the Younger in 1818), and by 1850 only 70 such engines were coping with the drainage which had previously required 500 or so windmills.

The final stage of fen drainage which led to the recovery of some 600,000 acres of land began in the 20th century when the steam pumping stations were replaced by oil and later electrically powered pumps. From then onwards the water level could be accurately controlled by switches which brought the pumps into operation automatically, obviating the need for constant manning. But drainage is still vital with so much of the area below sea-level; if all the electric pumps were switched off it is calculated that within a few days the sea would reclaim most of the land of the Fens.

THE FEN DWELLERS

The draining of the Fens was by no means universally popular; the Adventurers and landowners stood to gain, but the Fen dwellers saw it merely as a reduction of the waters from which they earned a precarious living by fishing, eeling and wildfowling. From time to time groups of the Fenmen known as the Fen Tigers rioted and destroyed the work carried out by the Undertakers so as to delay the drainage. The University authorities at Cambridge also opposed the drainage, claiming that their members would have nowhere to hunt and fish for relaxation, and consequently their health would suffer

THE FENS TODAY

The viability of the agricultural economy in the Fens is nowadays uncertain. The 60 ft-deep peat beds which provided such rich agricultural land have now shrunk in many places to only 4 or 5 ft. 'Fen Blows', strong and persistent winds which, particularly in spring, strip off top-soil, seeds and fertiliser, add to the problems. Shrinkage also leads to house-building problems on the recovered land, and even houses built on piled foundations still tend to need periodic structural repair.

However, while it is still there, the dark, rich, peat soil provides some of the best agricultural land in England. Wheat, barley, sugar beet, potatoes and carrots are the main crops grown, but fruit, salad vegetables and flowers are also produced. Bulbs are an important crop in certain parts of the Fens, and indeed bulb growing has been so successful that a large proportion of the bulbs grown are sold to the Netherlands.

Very little traditional fenland now remains, the best-known area being Wicken Fen about 10 miles north-east of Cambridge. This is managed as a nature reserve by the National Trust and is popular with naturalists who come to look at the birds and insects as well as the plants. Sites such as the Ouse Washes, where the land between the Old and New Bedford Rivers is seasonally flooded, also provide vital habitats for wildfowl and other birds.

The City
Its History

For many people the name 'Cambridge' conjures up a picture of an ancient university around which a town has grown. The truth is different; Cambridge was a small prosperous town 1,000 years before the 'coming of the clerks'.

EARLY SETTLEMENT
In the 1st century AD the Romans built a road between their fortified towns at Colchester and Chester, which forded the river now known as the Cam very close to the site of the present-day Magdalene Street Bridge in Cambridge. The higher land to the north (Castle Hill) provided an ideal site for a fort from which to defend the river crossing. Around the fort a small civilian settlement grew.

The small town prospered under the Romans, but when the Legions were withdrawn from Britain early in the 5th century AD, it declined rapidly and for a time the settlement was almost deserted.

The Roman name for the town is not known for certain, though it may have been *Camboritum*. Other early records give the name as *Grantabryce* (with a variety of spellings), then *Grauntbryce* and *Cauntbridge*. By the 15th century, however, the present-day names for town and river, Cambridge and the Cam, were in use.

AFTER THE ROMANS
The year AD450 saw an invasion of England by the Saxons and Jutes, Germanic tribes from the Rhine Valley area. They came to raid and rob, but stayed on to farm and settle in East Anglia. Some early Saxons occupied the site of the old Roman fort at Cambridge, but others started building on the gravel beds which rose above the marshes south of the river. A second settlement grew up here (now the Bene't Street and Market Square area). The name *Lorthburg* or *Lurtheburg* has been given to this village, based on old records which refer to Lortberg Lane in the middle of the settlement.

BRONZE GILT
An Anglo-Saxon brooch found near Cambridge

THE DANES
In the 6th and 7th centuries AD East Anglia was overrun by the Danes and Norsemen from Scandinavia. There followed two centuries of conflict between the English and the new invaders (who were seeking to expand their lands), which ended in 878 when King Alfred defeated the Danes at Ethendune and imposed the Treaty of Wedmore. This treaty effectively confined the Danes to a part of eastern England known as the Danelaw.

The Danes were a seafaring and trading nation, and saw that Cambridge would make an ideal inland port. They built a wooden bridge over the river in about AD750 and established quays on the eastern bank of the Cam between their 'Great Bridge' (at Magdalene Street) and

TRADING PLACE
Below: Stourbridge Fair

the Silver Street area. Trade goods were brought across the North Sea and offloaded at Lynn (King's Lynn) from where they were transported inland along the rivers Ouse and Cam. These river communications, together with road links (two ancient Roman roads, *Via Devana* and Akeman Street, crossed close to the port area), enabled Cambridge to become a wealthy town. Most early buildings were made of wood, but in the early 11th century the citizens were prosperous enough to build a stone tower for the Church of St Bene't.

Because the southern village, *Lorthburg*, was closer to the quays than the older town, it soon became the dominant settlement. It was here that a market-place was established, and later the guild and municipal offices. Eventually, however, the two settlements merged into one another.

NORMAN AND MEDIEVAL CAMBRIDGE

Soon after the Norman invasion of England in 1066, William the Conqueror built a wooden motte and bailey castle on the site of the Roman fort at Castle Hill. This was built as a headquarters to control the local population and suppress any revolt from Hereward the Wake and his 'Islanders' at Ely (see page 11), and it is doubtful whether it was ever used as a royal residence.

William's great survey of England, the *Domesday Book* of 1086, showed Cambridge to be a flourishing and important commercial centre with about 400 houses. The Normans encouraged the town's development, and much building took place. The 'Round Church' and the School of Pythagoras, home of the town's first mayor, are two buildings dating from this period (see page 22).

The reign of William II (or Rufus) saw the establishment of the first religious house in the town. An Augustinian monastery was founded in 1092 on the site of today's St Giles' Church at the Castle Street/Chesterton Lane junction. Other denominations soon followed and the religious communities were granted various rights to hold annual fairs, the fees and dues from which supported the house.

In this way Stourbridge Fair, held on the common of that name on the north-east outskirts of the town, came to play a major role in the development of trade in Cambridge. In 1211 King John granted the fair to the Hospital for Lepers, the chapel of which still stands on the Newmarket Road (A45). The proximity of the fairground to the river encouraged merchants from the Continent to trade at Stourbridge, and it rapidly became the largest fair in Europe. It declined in importance in the 18th century and was ended by royal decree in 1933, but its memory is preserved in John Bunyan's *Vanity Fair* which is based on the excesses of the fair.

The origins of the University are probably closely tied to the religious houses and fairs, as monks would have been attracted to the town to preach and teach. However, the date usually given for the foundation of the University is 1209, the year when a group of students, escaping from riots in Oxford, set themselves up in Cambridge (see page 17).

TOWN AND UNIVERSITY

By the late 14th century the University had become a powerful force in Cambridge and, although the first scholars had been made welcome, the townspeople had developed a deep-rooted hatred of the University and its members. The townspeople's complaint was that although the town had held a Royal Charter since 1100, which had been confirmed by King John in 1205, their elected mayor had to swear an oath to maintain the rights and privileges of the University and to yield precedence to the Vice-Chancellor at all times.

The Peasants' Revolt of 1381 saw at least one college plundered by the townsmen who then compelled the Vice-Chancellor to sign away all the privileges and rights that the University held. However, the Bishop of Norwich, with armed troops, entered Cambridge, put down the riots and hanged the five ringleaders. Richard II then restored all the University's rights and privileges and punished the town heavily. It was not until the 19th century that the University eventually gave up many of its rights over

TOWN HERALDRY
The town's coat of arms, granted in 1575, shows the importance of river trade in Cambridge's history

. . .Historic characters depicted on an early 19th-century handbill

FORMER SKYLINE
Cambridge in the 1740s. King's College and the tower of Great St Mary's show up well

Petty Cury, in 1909, before many of its rich medley of buildings from past ages were demolished

the town, and disputes between 'Town and Gown' flared up periodically over the intervening 500 years.

CAMBRIDGE AND ROYALTY

Although it has seldom been at the centre of national affairs, a number of monarchs have visited the town over the years, and on at least one occasion (in the late 14th century) a parliament was held there. In 1553 it was the setting for the proclamation of Lady Jane Grey as Queen of England. However, the Duke of Northumberland, then Chancellor of the University, who made the proclamation did not realise that Mary Tudor, Henry VIII's daughter, was at nearby Sawston Hall. The following day Mary Tudor was proclaimed Queen in London, and although the Duke himself then proclaimed Mary in Cambridge, he was arrested in King's College Chapel and subsequently executed.

In the 17th century Cambridge again played a major role in national events. The teaching of 16th-century churchmen such as Latimer, Ridley and Cranmer (all of whom preached Reform from Cambridge pulpits and paid with their lives at Oxford) led to the rise of the Commonwealth Party and the subsequent beheading of Charles I. Oliver Cromwell, sometime student of Sidney Sussex College, and a Member of Parliament for Cambridge, became the Lord Protector of England. Cambridge commanded the crossing point of routes between East Anglia and the Midlands, and so the town became the Headquarters of the Eastern Counties Association, an armed force set up to defend the area against the King's Army. Cromwell strengthened the Norman castle with stone bought by Clare College for a rebuilding scheme. At the same time he demolished all the bridges over the River Cam except for the Great Bridge. Despite Cambridge's importance in the Commonwealth the University was largely Royalist, and the restoration of the monarch in 1660 was celebrated with red wine flowing from the fountain on the Market Square.

17th- AND 18th-CENTURY DEVELOPMENTS

In the mid 17th century road links with London were improved and the first regular coach service between the towns started in 1653. The year 1724 saw the passing of an Act of Parliament which authorised Turnpike Trusts to collect a fee from road users for the maintenance of the highway. The engraved stone marking the point at which the Godmanchester turnpike road ended can still be seen on the wall of No 8 Castle Street.

This period also saw the development of various social amenities. Early in the 17th century Dr Stephen Perse left money in his will to found a free school to educate 100 boys and to build almshouses. Both are still in use though on new sites. A century and a half later, in 1766, the famous teaching hospital named after Dr John Addenbrooke, a Fellow of St Catharine's College, was opened.

A BISHOP AND A STATESMAN
Hugh Latimer (top), c.1485–1555, and Oliver Cromwell, 1599–1658— two famous names from Cambridge's history

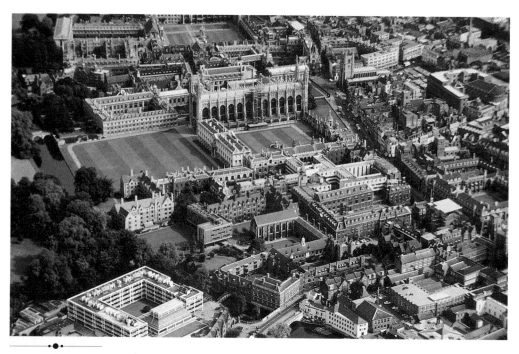

THE TOWN IN WARTIME
The Bull Hotel was used by American troops stationed in Cambridge during World War II

THE 19th AND 20th CENTURIES

The Reform Act of 1832 put an end to many municipal excesses. It followed an enquiry by a Royal Commission which found Cambridge to be one of the most corrupt boroughs in England. The affairs of 20,000 people were controlled by only 158 freemen with voting rights, who apparently had no hesitation in spending £1,300 on dinners at the same time as providing only £480 for council services and road repairs.

The Victorian period saw the arrival of the railway in Cambridge, with the consequent development of more speedy communications. However, the University authorities decreed that the station must be a suitable distance away from the colleges, hence its location in the south-east of the town a couple of miles away from the city centre.

Later in the 19th century a large Corn Exchange was constructed for the county's farmers, and the town also opened a free public library and reading room.

Like most other towns, Cambridge lost many of its young men in World War I. Even so, there was much unemployment in the town in the 1920s. Government funds brought some relief in allowing the construction of bridges—a footbridge over the Cam in the north-west of the city linking Pretoria Road with Midsummer Common, and a series of bridges across Coe Fen and Sheep's Green from Trumpington Road to Newnham. The road across these bridges, Fen Causeway, was expected to be a waste of money as no one would need to use it. Today, however, it is one of the city's busiest roads.

A boundary expansion took place in 1934 when large areas of Trumpington and Cherry Hinton were added to the town, increasing the area to more than 10,000 acres. Between the wars four major new schools were built to accommodate the increasing numbers of children, evening classes for adults became popular, and two new branch libraries were built in the suburbs.

World War II caused the number of students in the town to diminish rapidly as they were called up, but the vacated college accommodation was soon filled by trainees for the Forces, mainly RAF. The town acquired many evacuees of all ages, some of whom stayed on after the war. A certain amount of damage to property was caused by bombing, and a number of people were killed, but fortunately Cambridge never became a military target in spite of its surrounding aerodromes and 6,000 trainee airmen.

The period since the war has seen a steady rise in industry and building in the city. Much of the industry has been in the scientific and hi-tech fields and more Science and Business Parks are being opened on the outskirts of the city. These enable small firms to set up in pleasant surroundings and to make use of the scientific and other specialised skills available within the University departments.

Observant readers may have noted that despite the title of this article, Cambridge has generally been referred to as a 'town' rather than a 'city'. This is because despite its size (with a population of over 100,000) the town of Cambridge was only elevated to city status in 1951.

Beautiful college buildings and peaceful courtyards, traditions and privileges are the hallmarks of the University of Cambridge, but today this ancient seat of learning—an amalgamation of colleges, faculties, libraries and museums—is also a leading scientific research centre.

THE EARLY YEARS

The origin of the University in Cambridge is unknown, but it is generally considered to date from 1209, when a group of students who had been driven out of Oxford by serious rioting came to Cambridge to continue their studies. They may have arrived with the intention of setting up a 'School', but it is rather more likely that they came to one already established.

A 'University' in its simplest form was a body of learned men gathered together for the purpose of teaching. These men, the 'Masters', would only allow people to teach once they were satisfied as to their abilities. The licence to teach was known as a 'Degree', and degree holders were permitted to teach in any part of the country. Following a Papal Bull of 1318, Cambridge was declared a *studium generale* or place of general education, which meant that degree holders could teach in any Christian country.

The early University had no money of its own, nor did it own property. The principal study was theology, requiring much of the scholars' time to be spent in devotions, and local churches provided for this need. Religious houses and churches were also used as lecture rooms and for University ceremonies.

HOSTELS

Unless a scholar studying at Cambridge was a member of a religious house, it was necessary for him to provide for his own board and lodgings, and usually he would reside with a family in town. This caused certain problems: the young students (usually only 14 or 15 years old) were frequently accused of being ill-disciplined, and the landlords often saw students as a ready source of income and overcharged them.

As a result it became increasingly common for Masters and their scholars to band together to purchase or hire a local house in which they lived a communal life. The larger of these houses became known as 'hostels', and at times there were as many as 27 hostels in the town. However, such hostels did not solve the problems of youths of scholastic ability who lacked the money necessary to stay in Cambridge for seven years in order to reach Degree standard. The late 13th and 14th centuries saw the emergence of benefactors who, for the salvation of their souls, were willing to provide charitable funds to support such scholars.

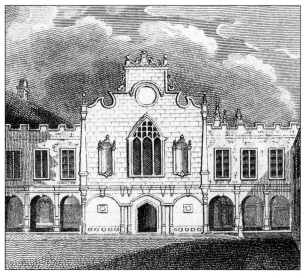

THE COLLEGES

In 1280 Hugh de Balsham, the Bishop of Ely, decided to install a group of student monks in Cambridge to enable them to study and attend public lectures. He was no doubt prompted by the establishment, 16 years earlier, of Merton College, a house for maintained scholars in Oxford. The young monks from Ely were housed at the Hospital of St John in Cambridge, a charitable foundation where old and infirm men were nursed by some of the older Ely monks. Unfortunately, the young monks were unable to live peaceably with the older brothers, and in 1284 Balsham acquired two tenements outside the southern boundary of the town and installed his scholars there. The tithes of St Peter's Church were used to support his college, and when Balsham died two years later he left money which enabled the college to buy land and erect a hall, St Peter's College or Peterhouse.

As this college was maintained by the Bishop of Ely, only monks from Ely could live there. However, Balsham's foundation encouraged others, and in the 70 years following the establishment of Peterhouse five new collegiate foundations appeared. There then followed a space of almost 100 years, a time of plague and public unrest, before 1441 when Henry VI founded his college dedicated as 'The King's College of the Blessed Virgin and St Nicholas' and now known as King's College. Another nine colleges arose by 1594, but then there was another lull until around 1800 when Downing College was founded.

Today there are 31 colleges established in Cambridge, including three which were founded for ladies. The first of these (Girton) started life at Hitchin in 1869 and transferred to its Huntingdon Road site in 1872. In the late 1960s some of the men's colleges began to accept women, and this led to a rise in the number of female students in the University. Women now comprise 39 per cent of the total student population of around 12,000.

ADMINISTRATION OF THE UNIVERSITY AND COLLEGES

As stated already, the University is defined as the 'Chancellor, Masters and Scholars', but the decision-making or executive power is in the hands of the Regent House. This body consists of all residential Masters of Art (or MAs)—essentially the teaching and research staff of the University—and is too large for effective administration. University business is therefore first discussed in the Council of the Senate (whose members are elected from the Regent House), and its decisions and recommendations are then passed on to the Regent House for final approval. *Ad hoc* committees are formed to advise the Council on specialised matters, and experts in the appropriate field are invited to serve on such committees.

The head of the University, or Chancellor, is usually a person holding high public office (the present incumbent is Prince Philip), and the day-to-day business is conducted by the Vice-Chancellor who is the head of one of the colleges. The post of Vice-Chancellor is held for two years.

The governing body of a college consists of the Master and Fellows (the senior teaching and administrative staff), but here, too, power is vested in the College Council, selected by vote from the college's residential MAs.

FINANCE

The University is financed in part by Government grant, in part by money from national and international research

'THE RUGGER MAN'
Rugby is one of ten sports in which students may be awarded a 'Full Blue'

Trinity Hall's coat of arms plus that of William Bateman, Bishop of Norwich, who founded the college in the mid 14th century

agencies, and in part by payments levied on the colleges based on an elaborate system of taxation. Money also comes from endowments, some ancient and some modern. Industries and commerce may, in addition, finance research and even endow Professorships, but despite this only the utmost frugality on the part of the Board of Finance allows so much research to be carried on in Cambridge.

The colleges receive no state aid and are funded by bequests and student fees. Some, having owned land and property over many centuries, are very rich; others are much poorer. However, there is a good relationship between all the colleges, the wealthier ones contributing money to the 'University Chest' on which the less wealthy colleges can draw for special items of expenditure.

COATS OF ARMS
The shields of Magdalene (top) and Pembroke colleges

CHANGING TIMES
Installation of the Duke of Northumberland as Chancellor in 1842. The 19th century was a time of great change as University reform slowly took place

Rich decoration and furnishing in an undergraduate's room at Trinity College photographed in 1911

THE FACULTIES

In early days the University provided a degree course in two parts which took seven years to complete. The Trivium (first three years of study) included grammar, logic and rhetoric. This was followed by the Quadrivium, with arithmetic, geometry, astronomy and music. New subjects were included in the course of studies from time to time, and particular encouragement to expanding the curriculum was provided by Prince Albert, Chancellor from 1847.

The first endowed Cambridge Professorship (or Chair) was that in Divinity founded by Lady Margaret Beaufort, the mother of Henry VII, in 1502. Since then Chairs have been founded by public benefactors and by past members of the University in many subjects. Around the Professorships, departments, grouped into 20 faculties, have grown. A wide range of subjects are now taught and researched, ranging from physics (where Cambridge has produced many of the famous names of the 20th century—see page 31) to oriental studies, architecture and the history of art, and criminology. Research students are attached to particular departments, but undergraduates, though attending lectures and sitting examinations provided by the University, are supervised and tutored by their colleges.

OTHER UNIVERSITY FACILITIES

In addition to the lecture halls, libraries, laboratories and offices of the departments, the University also administers a number of museums. These are used by the students in connection with their studies but most are also open to the public. Several, including the Museum of Archaeology and Anthropology, the Museum of Zoology, and the Sedgwick Museum of Geology, are to be found in the Downing Street area. Nearby, in Free School Lane, is the Whipple Museum of the History of Science. Other University facilities include the Botanic Garden and the Fitzwilliam Museum, both well worth a visit (see city gazetteer).

UNIVERSITY SPORTS

Students of old were considered to be at college just to study, and sporting activities were not encouraged. Football and 'such like rowdy games' were frowned upon, and there are references in some University histories to scholars being forbidden to play marbles on the steps of the Senate House. Play acting, circuses and bear baiting required a licence from the Vice-Chancellor if the performance was to be within five miles of the University. But each college had its bowling green, bowls being the only officially approved sport.

Today's students are given every opportunity to take part in a wide range of sports including tennis, rugby, rowing and even tiddly-winks. For some, there may be the chance of a 'Blue', awarded to those representing the University in Oxford versus Cambridge sporting encounters.

VENERABLE MASTER
William Gretton, Master of Magdalene College, caricatured in 1809

IN FULL SPATE
Left: a richly carved Doric-style centre-piece dominates the Senate House where Professor Willis is seen lecturing to the Archaeological Institute

COLLEGE HERALDRY
St John's (top) and King's College coats of arms

King's College Chapel

The Chapel of King's College is world famous, and each year hundreds of thousands of people visit it and walk beneath its magnificent vaulted ceiling. Millions more know of it through the annual broadcasts of the Festival of Nine Lessons and Carols on Christmas Eve.

Stained-glass near the Chapel entrance

THE EARLY DAYS OF THE CHAPEL

The beautiful Gothic building was begun in 1446 by Henry VI who, at the age of 19 years, founded King's College of which the Chapel is a part. The civil strife of the Wars of the Roses slowed down the building of the Chapel, and it was 70 years before even all the walls and roof were complete. Construction took place during the reigns of five monarchs and was finally completed in the middle years of the 16th century.

In 1461, 10 years after the civil war broke out, Henry VI was overthrown. At this time only the first four bays from the east had been completed. The Yorkist Kings, Edward IV and Richard III, carried on with the Chapel to the original design and at the time of Richard's defeat at the Battle of Bosworth Field in 1485 seven bays were completed to roof height, four of which were roofed enabling the eastern end to be used.

Building work came almost to a standstill in the latter part of the 15th century as to start with the new king, Henry Tudor (Henry VII), took no interest in the Chapel. However, by the beginning of the 16th century its founder,

Henry VI, was being regarded as a saint, and Henry Tudor thought that his hold on the Crown might be strengthened by a public display of his support for his predecessor. On St George's Day 1506 he visited Cambridge and gave the sum of £5,000 towards the cost of construction. In addition he undertook to provide sufficient further money to ensure the Chapel's completion. On Henry VII's death in 1509 his executors provided funds for finishing the building, leaving only the furnishings to be provided.

In 1512 the master mason John Wastell was appointed, and he signed a contract to construct a vaulted ceiling at a cost of £100 per bay with a contract time of three years. Wastell's vaulting is of the 'fan' variety, and is breathtaking in its lightness and beauty. Notice that in the Chapel the fans spring from corbels half-way up the wall, whereas in the Ante-Chapel the fans spread from columns with their bases on the floor.

The stone used for the first stage of the Chapel was a white magnesian limestone, transported by water from a quarry near Tadcaster in Yorkshire. Delays in building, and probably financial considerations, led to the Chapel being completed in an oolitic limestone quarried near Northampton. This is a darker rock, and a look at the buttresses on both the north and south sides of the building shows clearly how far work had progressed at the time of Henry VI's overthrow in 1461. The change in stone is most noticeable at the bases of the two western turrets.

ADDING THE FINAL TOUCHES

With the walls and roof finished by 1515, the College approached the young Henry VIII for help in furnishing the Chapel. Henry responded by granting money to provide the windows, flooring, organ screen and stalls.

Installation of the windows began in 1515 and continued until 1545, although the west window, depicting the Last Judgement, was not put in until 1879. The medieval windows, in an arrangement known as type and anti-type, depict scenes from the New Testament in the lower half, and related scenes from the Old Testament in the upper sections. A number of designers worked on the windows, the best known being the King's Glaziers, Barnard Flowers and Galyon Hone.

The oak organ screen in fine Renaissance style covered with intricate

HARMONIOUS
EXTERIOR
*The east end of the Chapel
and the adjoining screen
wall as seen from King's
Parade*

carvings is a tribute to the wood carver's art. It was constructed before 1536 while Henry VIII was married to Anne Boleyn, and bears the couples' initials, H and A, above the entrance. The choir stalls are of a similar age to the organ screen, although the hoods above and the carvings are of a later period, having been commissioned in 1633. Also of a later date are the screen gates which bear the coat of arms of Charles I and the date 1633.

The first organ was installed in 1606 and was replaced in 1688 by a Renatus Harris organ. This, too, has been enlarged and rebuilt on several occasions.

THE CHAPEL IN THE
20th CENTURY

Fortunately the Chapel survived the ravages of two world wars intact. The windows, probably the best complete collection of medieval windows in the country, were removed to a place of safety before World War II. Their replacement was started in 1948 and it took five years to put back the 1,300 square yards of glass.

The altar piece, the *Adoration of the Magi* by Peter Paul Rubens, was given to the College in 1961 and, some 10 years later, the eastern end of the Chapel was altered by lowering the altar steps so that the Rubens could be displayed to the best advantage. The painting can now be viewed through the organ screen arch from the west end of the Chapel.

THE CHAPEL CHOIR

The choir still consists of 16 boys as ordered by Henry VI but nowadays it is augmented by 14 male voices. Famous past members of the choir include Orlando Gibbons who composed madrigals and motets in the 17th century. The choir boys can often be seen in the afternoon when, dressed in top hats, Eton jackets, striped trousers and gowns, they march in a

'crocodile' from their school to the Chapel for rehearsals or services.

VISITING THE CHAPEL

There is a minimum of unobtrusive low-power electric lighting in the Chapel and Ante-Chapel, but the real glory of the interior can best be appreciated when the candles are lit for the evening service in winter, and the walls and fan-vaulting recede into a shimmer of candle-light. Most of the services in term-time are open to the public; the times are displayed on a notice board in the south porch.

There is a bookstall from which postcards, guide books and recordings of the choir can be obtained, but it closes 30 minutes before services. There is also an exhibition of the history and construction of the Chapel in the small chapels on the north side, and the modest entrance fee to this and proceeds from the bookstall go towards the upkeep and maintenance of the building.

THE CHOIR
*The brass lectern (top) in
front of the choir stalls was
presented to the Chapel in
the early 16th century*

*The Chapel's 16 choir boys,
together with other pupils,
are educated at King's
College School, founded in
the 15th century*

A Selection
of
Architecture

Cambridge can provide a complete history of English architecture. The oldest surviving building dates back to before the Norman Conquest of 1066 and each succeeding style of architecture can be found somewhere within the town and university areas of the city. Modern architecture is well represented too, if not universally well-liked, and much of it is in the international prize-winning bracket.

CHURCH TOWERS
The squat Saxon tower of St Bene't's Church displays long and short work on the corners of the rubble walls

Above and right: the circular tower and cone of the Round Church are 19th-century restoration work, replacing a 15th-century polygonal bell-tower

THE OLDER BUILDINGS

The oldest building still standing in Cambridge is the tower of St Bene't's Church in Bene't Street, just off King's Parade. Thought to have been built a little before 1050, it displays, both inside and out, the proportions and features of pre-Conquest, or Saxon, building. The walls are very thick at the base, getting a little thinner each time as they rise through three stages. The stones at each corner form an irregular pattern known as 'long and short work', and the main window openings have somewhat crudely carved round-headed arches cut into massive blocks of stone supported by sturdy baluster shafts. Most of the church was heavily restored in the 19th century, and the aisles were rebuilt at this time.

The Church of the Holy Sepulchre, more commonly known as the Round Church, stands towards the town end of Bridge Street. This is one of only four surviving round churches in the country. The circular nave and aisle were built in the first half of the 12th century together with a small rectangular chancel which

was enlarged in the 13th century and again in the 15th century. In 1841 the eminent architect Anthony Salvin was highly praised for his restoration of the church; today many people think that it was very much overdone. However, there is much original and restored work to admire and enjoy inside the building. The most interesting original Norman work is the lower level of the nave where eight solid columns with roll-moulded arches link with the rib-vaulted ceiling of the aisles.

All the other medieval churches in the city have interesting features which record the constant remodelling that was practised from the 11th through to the 16th centuries. Today we are so used to accepting these buildings as we find them, that it is difficult to appreciate how revolutionary the introduction of new styles would have been at the time.

The most visually interesting of the older secular buildings is the School of Pythagoras in St John's College. It is one of those great rarities—a two-storeyed stone-built Norman house. The older, round-headed windows indicate a late 12th-century age. The shafts and capitals are in the transitional fashion developing from the Norman into the Early English style. Entrance to the original building would have been on the first floor by an outside staircase to a door at the east gable end, but by the 14th century doorways had been inserted at ground level.

Cambridge has more timber-framed buildings than are at first obvious, and many of the smaller buildings still to be seen in the city centre were constructed in this way. Most of them hide behind remodelled façades of brick-casing or stuccoed rendering, but there are some that reveal all. Bridge Street, between the bridge and the Round Church, proudly boasts some very fine buildings. Bridge House, which has a passage-way leading through to a multi-storey car park, is double-jettied, which means that the two upper floors project. The timber revealed is expansive and expensive.

There are three other timber-framed buildings in the city also worth closer inspection, namely the Folk Museum at the bottom of Castle Street, west of the river, the Varsity Restaurant in St Andrew's Street, and the Little Rose, a pub opposite the Fitzwilliam Museum in Trumpington Street. All would have been

*The timber frame of the Folk Museum sets off a
display of May Day garlands*

situated outside the main part of medieval
Cambridge, although there had for a long
time been a settlement in the area around
the Folk Museum.

Cloister Court in Queens' College
shows both timber and brick construction.
Three sides of the court have 15th-century
brick; an extremely expensive material in
those days. The fourth side confirms the
court's picturesque quality with the
immaculate timberwork of the President's
Gallery. Legend has these timbers coming
from ships, but that is most unlikely as it
was, and still is, virtually impossible to
remodel saltwater-seasoned wood.

King's College Chapel (described in
greater detail elsewhere—see page 20) is,
of course, the most magnificent example
of the ultimate of English Gothic style, the
Perpendicular period of the late 15th and
early 16th centuries.

17th-CENTURY BUILDINGS
The mid 17th century brought a distinct
change of architectural style to England,
which, in Cambridge, is reflected in the
work of Christopher Wren. Wren's
Pembroke College Chapel of 1665 is the
earliest of Cambridge's purely classical
buildings. Three years later he produced
Emmanuel College Chapel, and in 1676
began Trinity College Library (commonly
known as the Wren Library), the most
visually peaceful of buildings. The
Fellows' Building at Christ's College,
begun in 1640, the inner ranges of the
main court of St Catharine's College,
dating to the 1670s, and the Pepys
Building at Magdalene, which was
certainly there by 1688 (the date on the
façade, 1724, commemorates the arrival of
Pepys' library), are other superb secular
examples of the period. Clare College by
itself provides us with a history of
architectural development in the second
half of the century. In addition, the way
that the light plays on the intriguing
patterns of the south wall, when viewed
from King's College bridge, is well worth
seeing.

**ABOVE
EYE-LEVEL**
*Interesting architectural
details on Pembroke
College's classical chapel,
designed by Christopher
Wren and funded by his
uncle, Matthew Wren*

**A DIARIST'S
COLLECTION**
*On his death in 1703 Pepys
bequeathed his books to his
old college Magdalene, to be
kept in a room in the 'New
Building'. His motto and
the date the library was
installed were added later*

GREEK AND GOTHIC REVIVAL
William Wilkins' early 19th-century Greek Revival style at Downing College and the wide lawns help to give the college a feeling of spaciousness and classical simplicity

A close-up of buildings on King's Parade showing some of Wilkins' Gothic Revival work

18th-CENTURY BUILDINGS

The south side of the Front Court of Emmanuel College is graced with the much-acclaimed Westmorland Building of the first quarter of the century. It is a pleasant enough building but does not have the charm of two smaller contemporary town-houses, Fitzwilliam House (opposite the Fitzwilliam Museum) and Little Trinity (in Jesus Lane), which is a favourite of many people. Little Trinity was remodelled from an early 17th-century house, and the steep pitch of roof, the parapet, the symmetrical distribution of sash-windows, and the excellent door-casing, all combine to produce a splendid looking façade.

About the same time that these domestic houses were being built, James Gibbs was designing more formal buildings for the University and for King's College. The Senate House, in King's Parade opposite Great St Mary's Church, presents an elegant catalogue of classical features and decoration and the cornice beneath the balustraded parapet is a wonder of craftsmanship. Gibbs' Fellows' Building at King's can be admired from both the town and the river sides of the college. It is a plain, very restrained building that contrasts with the elaborate Gothic decoration of its neighbours.

19th-CENTURY BUILDINGS

The latter years of the previous century had been very quiet in Cambridge with little expansion occurring. The 19th century proved a complete contrast and a time of great vitality. With the number of undergraduates almost trebling in the first 30 years of the century, many new college buildings were constructed and there is a feast of architecture for the gourmet.

Of all the eminent architects to contribute to the Cambridge scene at this time William Wilkins was the most prolific. Most of his work is in the Gothic Revival style. It can be seen in the New Court at Trinity College, the Second Court at Corpus Christi College, and in many of the buildings around the Great Court of King's College, namely the Screen and Gateway, beside King's Parade, and the Hall Range, opposite the Chapel. In complete contrast is his Greek Revival of 1807 at Downing College with its spread of pavilions within a wide, lawned area. This was the earliest of all university campuses anywhere in the world.

Another piece of Gothic Revival architecture that has inspired followers is the New Building at St John's College. This is a large symmetrical building, surmounted by a tower with a cupola in the Gothic style, with a court enclosed by a screen. It is linked with the older courts by the so-called Bridge of Sighs. All these were built between 1825 and 1831 by Thomas Rickman and Henry Hutchinson. The final choice of 19th-century college building is Alfred Waterhouse's 1870s rebuilding of Tree Court at Gonville and Caius College.

To complete the 19th-century selection is one church and one commercial building. George Bodley designed All Saints Church in 1865. It is a very fine and elegant piece of Gothic Revival, set off by its well-proportioned tower and spire. A feature of note is the interior decoration by William Morris. Opposite Petty Cury on Sidney Street is Lloyds Bank Chambers. Alfred Waterhouse with Paul, his son and partner, designed the greater part of it in 1891; the rest dates to 1935.

Niches in Waterhouse's Tree Court at Caius contain statues of famous figures associated with the college

THE MODERN BUILDINGS

It is very easy to condemn, criticise and complain, and collect a sympathetic ear where recent 20th-century architecture is concerned. When it comes to accepting new design most of us reveal rather conservative traits. We sometimes overlook the fact that all earlier buildings were at one time modern, and that many were very avant-garde in their day.

The big central tower of the 1931—4 University Library by Sir Giles Gilbert Scott dominates the Cambridge skyline. A theme of vertical strips against a less obvious horizontal line dominates the whole building. The pale russet brickwork fades to a muddy grey in most lights giving it an impersonal air. The Sidgwick Site of faculty offices, libraries, lecture rooms and a museum brings together the work of a number of architects. The variety of shapes and materials are linked together by the controlled space between and sometimes beneath the buildings. The problems that hit James Stirling's prize-winning History Faculty, 1964—8, with collapsing cladding, and difficulties with the heating and the ventilation, tend to make people wary of new materials. One can imagine Gillespie, Kidd and Coia's Robinson College, of 1980, maturing in the manner of other and older brick-built colleges; yet, one has doubts about the concrete-clad colleges.

Two of the newer commercial buildings provide similar points of comparison. Anyone driving along the M11 close to Cambridge is bound to see the great marquee-like structure that dominates the High Cross site just off Madingley Road. Completed in 1985 and designed by John Hopkins, the Schlumberger Building has a very temporary look. Despite the sturdy forms of its posts and bracework it looks no more permanent than a circus tent. The teflon-coated glass-fibre of the canopy already shows a canvas-like discolouring. The glass-faced office cabins along the sides seem all ready for container

shipment. Nevertheless, despite these criticisms, it is a very exciting piece of architecture. Equally exciting, but with a feeling of reliable permanence, is the Napp Building on the Science Park off Milton Road. This can be seen and approached from the A45 dual-carriageway. Designed by Arthur Erickson and Partners, building began in 1981. It uses sloping buttress-like columns, cast in Spanish dolomite aggregate, and panels of reflective insulated glass. Inside and out the building glows with quality.

The Open Spaces
of
Cambridge

PARKER'S PIECE
*Today and at the time of
Queen Victoria's
Coronation Dinner in 1838
(inset)*

Cambridge is fortunate in the survival of so much green, open space where visitors and residents alike can walk or simply sit and watch the world go by. Many of these areas also have backdrops of fine buildings to delight the eye.

DINNER GIVEN to 15,000 Persons on PARKER'S PIECE, CAMBRIDGE in the presence of 25,000 Spectators
Thursday 28th June 1838.
IN HONOUR OF THE CORONATION OF HER MOST GRACIOUS MAJESTY QUEEN VICTORIA.
To commemorate which unrivalled Public Festival this Print is dedicated to the Subscribers
by Thos Hallack
Honorary Secretary

THE BACKS

The lawns and gardens between the River Cam and the colleges, and the river and Queen's Road, are collectively known as the Backs and are, probably, Cambridge's best-known open space. They stretch from St John's College in the north, down to Queens' College in the south. Footpaths weave up and down across the Backs but, especially in summer, the best views can be obtained from a punt on the river. The Backs are also worth visiting in March and April for the displays of spring flowers.

Much of the attraction of the Backs is in the rich variety of architectural styles represented by the buildings bordering the lawns and the river. Starting in the north, St John's College displays the neo-Gothic façade of New Court, together with the 'Bridge of Sighs' which joins the two parts of the college. Then comes Trinity College with Sir Christopher Wren's library, Clare College with its classical south range, and King's College with its Gothic chapel and 'Great Lawn'. Further south still is Queens' College, and here it is the modern buildings, the sympathetic Erasmus Building and the stark, white Cripps Court which face the river.

OTHER RIVERSIDE COMMONS AND GREENS

The Backs are only a part of an arc of open spaces bordering the river, stretching from Stourbridge Common at the north-east of the city to the meadows down towards Grantchester to the south.

Often the names of these open spaces are fascinating and informative. Coe Fen, in the south, for instance, gets its name from the jackdaw, or 'coo' in Old English. The name of the neighbouring Sheep's Green is fairly self-explanatory, while Lammas Land, also in the south-west part of the city, is so named because it was cleared at Lammas (1 August). These three areas, which are rather more 'rural' than the commons to the north of the city, have a number of nature trails crossing them and are used for grazing cattle and horses.

Where the river curves eastwards in the north of the city it encircles Jesus Green with its avenues of large plane trees and open-air swimming pool. Across Victoria Avenue is Midsummer Common, so-called from the fair held there at midsummer since the 13th century. Further east still along the river is Stourbridge Common, where Stourbridge Fair, 'the largest and most famous fair in all England', was held from King John's reign until the 1930s: Stourbridge was the steer, or ox bridge. Across Newmarket Road is Coldham's Common, the cold 'hamm' meaning meadow.

IDYLLIC SCENES
Views of King's College Chapel (far left) and Clare College from the Backs

THE CITY SQUARES

Within the city are a number of more formal open spaces, the largest of which is Parker's Piece. This was named after Edward Parker, a chef at Trinity College, who grazed cattle on the green in readiness for the table. The turrets of the University Arms Hotel in the north-west corner of the square loom over Hobbs' Pavilion, a memorial to the Cambridge cricketer Jack Hobbs who achieved 197 centuries and more than 61,000 runs during his first-class cricket career. The Pavilion, erected in 1928, is now a restaurant specialising in pancakes. Parker's Piece is much used by local sports clubs, as well as being the site for the opening carnival of the Cambridge City Festival, and nearby are other sports facilities, the Kelsey Kerridge Sports Hall and Parkside Swimming Pool, and Fenner's, the University cricket ground.

Other smaller city squares include Christ's Pieces with its trees, flower beds, bowling green and tennis courts, at the back of the Bus Station, and New Square, adjoining it to the east. New Square has terraces of town-houses on three sides, built in the second quarter of the 19th century to a coherent design, but with interesting individual differences. Its charm has been restored now that the car park has gone and the area has been regrassed.

AT THE CREASE
The weathervane on top of the clock tower of Hobbs' Pavilion depicts the famous cricketer 'Jack' Hobbs, born in Cambridge in 1882

Famous Students

Over the years of its existence the university at Cambridge has, like any other university, produced large numbers of people who have led worthy (though not noteworthy) lives in such professions as the Church, teaching and administration. Others have achieved more lasting fame: as statesmen or martyrs, as scientists or entertainers.

OLIVERIVS CROMWEL. ANGLICÆ REIP. PRO-TECTOR. EIVSDEMQ. EXERCITWM DVX GENERALIS, ETC.

Nicholas Ridley (c.1500–1555). Ridley was a student and later Master at Pembroke College, and ended his life as a Protestant martyr

BISHOPS AND COURTIERS

The religious upheavals of the 16th century turned many Cambridge men into martyrs. Bishop John Fisher, the great benefactor who had instigated the founding of Christ's and St John's colleges, was executed in 1535. His 'crime' was to deny the claim asserted by Thomas Cranmer, that Henry VIII should be head of the Church in England. Cranmer himself had been a student at Jesus College, but nearly blighted his career by marrying. However, his wife died, so Cranmer returned to college, entered Holy Orders, became the king's chaplain and finally Archbishop of Canterbury. But in 1556 he died at the stake in Oxford on a charge of heresy. Shortly before his death he witnessed the burning at the stake of Bishops Ridley and Latimer, from Pembroke and Clare colleges respectively.

Although Cambridge continued to produce churchmen in large numbers, in the latter part of the century young aristocrats were also attracted to the University. Robert Devereux, Earl of Essex and later a favourite of Queen Elizabeth I, went to Cambridge when he was only 10 years old. He was placed in the care of the Master of Trinity College, but nevertheless managed to spend beyond his means and had to write a contrite letter to his guardian, Lord Burleigh.

THE PURITANS

Most students, however, came from humbler backgrounds. Oliver Cromwell's father was a gentleman of Huntingdon who, in 1616, sent his son to Sidney Sussex College. Cromwell was a student in Cambridge for only a year before his father's death necessitated his return home, but later he became Member of Parliament for the town and established his Eastern Counties Association there during the Commonwealth Period. In 1960, a head (almost certainly Cromwell's) was returned to his old college for reburial, but its exact whereabouts are kept secret.

John Milton, the great poet, was a student at Christ's College for seven years from 1625. He found himself at odds with his more frivolous companions, who nicknamed him 'The Lady' for his fastidious ways and smooth face. But he was not without a wry humour. When the local carrier Thomas Hobson died, Milton's epitaph for him described Death's pursuit along the London road.

In the early 17th century, many of

Robert Devereux, 2nd Earl of Essex, who was a Master of Arts by the age of 13

Cambridge's staunch Puritans sailed to New England where they could worship as they chose. In Cambridge, Massachusetts, they founded their own college, naming it after John Harvard, a benefactor who had recently arrived from Emmanuel College.

PEPYS AND NEWTON

Early in 1651 Samuel Pepys arrived at Magdalene College. His family came from Cottenham, near Cambridge, and some of his kin were officers of the town council. The college records mention Pepys only once, on the occasion when he was 'scandalously overseen in drink'. While a student, he spent some time writing a novel called *Love a Cheat* which in later years he tore up, though marvelling that he could have written so well. But it was as a book collector that Pepys made his lasting contribution to Cambridge, for he left his own superb library and bookcases to Magdalene. His famous shorthand diary, recording daily life in the 1660s, is also housed in the library.

Pepys came to know the most famous scientist ever to study at Cambridge, Isaac Newton. Even as a schoolboy Newton showed an unusual interest in things mechanical and scientific, and at Trinity College he distinguished himself as a mathematician, becoming a Fellow and then Professor of Mathematics. He lived most of his life in Cambridge, and though

Samuel Pepys Esq⟨r⟩. *Secretary to the* Admiralty.
From an Original by Sir Godfrey Kneller.

His Autograph from an original Letter in the possession of John Thane.

Samuel Pepys (1633–1703), who left his library of 3,000 volumes to his old college, Magdalene

he was actually at home in Lincolnshire when the famous incident of the falling apple is said to have occurred, the theory of gravity that resulted was written (in Latin) at Trinity. An apple tree by the college gate and a statue in the chapel commemorate him.

THOMAS GRAY AND THE ROPE-LADDER

In the 18th century, Cambridge was renowned, as Byron later put it, for its 'din and drunkenness'. To this world came Thomas Gray, a scrivener's son of refined tastes and quiet but biting wit. Gray decided to stay at Peterhouse, after taking a degree in law, to pursue his own interests in the classics, history and writing poetry. Nowadays he is, of course, best known for his *Elegy Written in a Country Churchyard*. To some of the undergraduates he was a figure of fun and they saw a wonderful opportunity for some sport when Gray had a rope-ladder installed in his top-floor room as a fire escape. On a February night the young men gave a false alarm after, some say, placing a tub of water beneath Gray's window. Whether he tumbled down his ladder into it is not recorded, but Gray was mortally affronted by this prank. When the Master of Peterhouse declined to punish the offenders, Gray removed to Pembroke College.

18th-CENTURY POLITICIANS

Another person connected with Pembroke was William Pitt (the Younger) who came up to the college as a boy of 14. Though so young and suffering ill health, Pitt's academic ability was recognised and he studied enthusiastically with his tutor until he left college in 1779. Within a year he had a seat in Parliament, and in the general election of 1784 he became

Member of Parliament for Cambridge University. He had already, at 24, been made Britain's youngest Prime Minister. After his death in 1806 he was commemorated in Cambridge by the University Press building in Trumpington Street (the Pitt Building) and a statue at Pembroke College.

A close friend and colleague of Pitt was William Wilberforce, his contemporary at St John's College. Wilberforce, who came from Hull, was an able and very sociable young man but even he thought it odd that his tutor should invite him straightaway to an evening's gambling. However, the combination of hard work and fun seemed to suit Wilberforce very well and was a way of life he continued into adulthood. From Cambridge he went into Parliament and there took up the case against slavery.

'A GLIMPSE OF CAM'

William Wordsworth, from distant Cumberland, was also a student at St John's College. He described later his arrival in Cambridge in 1787, how he

  . . . *caught,*
  While crossing Magdalene Bridge, a glimpse of Cam
  And at the Hoop alighted, famous inn.

His rooms were over the college kitchens and there he could hear not only the domestic hubbub but also the more dignified tones of 'Trinity's loquacious clock'. For a while, he said, he gave up the solitariness he had enjoyed as a boy in the Lakeland fells, and joined in the bustle of undergraduate life. He even admitted getting drunk while toasting Milton's memory in the poet's old room.

A year or two later Samuel Taylor Coleridge arrived at Jesus College. Although the lives of the two poets became bound up together, they met only after leaving Cambridge. Coleridge was in some ways a misfit in the University. Although a good classical student and writer he was, apparently, too interested in current affairs, too curious and not good enough at mathematics. Failing to achieve his ambitions, he ran away from Cambridge and enlisted in the Army as Silas Tompkins Comberbache. He was eventually found out and returned to Cambridge, but could not settle and left without a degree.

to reform Cambridge were being released. A greater sobriety amongst the undergraduates was encouraged by the evangelical vicar at Holy Trinity Church. Charles Simeon of King's College had barely graduated before obtaining the living and setting about preaching a more inspired gospel than was usual at the time. He particularly aimed to help the many other undergraduates destined for the Church, and his tea-parties became famous. There students could discuss the doctrines, practice and teaching of Christianity in a way not provided for by the University. Simeon was at Holy Trinity from 1782 till his death in 1836. He was buried in King's College Chapel.

Tennyson, like Wordsworth his predecessor as Poet Laureate, studied at Cambridge

A ROMANTIC POET
Noted for his eccentric and aristocratic behaviour rather than his scholastic ability, Byron was at Trinity College in the early 19th century

BYRON

The ultimate representative of unreformed Cambridge, of the system at its worst, must be George Lord Byron. As we have seen, he recognised Cambridge's shortcomings and exploited them for his own enjoyment. College Fellows were themselves often idle or drunk but many of them pursued any aristocrat or man of influence who might offer them employment elsewhere. Lords, even undergraduate lords, were given many privileges. Byron arrived at Trinity, in 1805, an overweight, slightly lame youth rejoicing in his new independence. He immediately ordered three dozen bottles of wine and arranged for his horse to be stabled in town. Byron delighted in taunting the Fellows, and on finding the college forbade the keeping of dogs within the grounds acquired a bear cub which he paraded through the courts quite legitimately. When asked about the bear's future he replied 'he shall sit for a fellowship'. Despite this sort of behaviour and long absences in London, Byron was still awarded the customary degree.

EVANGELISTS AND APOSTLES

While Byron's experience epitomised the old order, in the late 18th and early 19th centuries the energies of those who wished

University reform was a very slow process and when Alfred Tennyson arrived in Cambridge in 1828 he could still observe sycophantic Fellows flattering young noblemen. Tennyson's first observations on Cambridge were not complimentary. He nevertheless found congenial friends and became one of the early associates of a society called the Apostles. Membership was by invitation and was extended only to those seen to be intellectually gifted and with open, inquiring minds. A measure of secrecy was observed about all the Society's affairs, and this is still so today. Tennyson was a published poet before going to Cambridge and there he continued to write, which cost him his degree.

EVOLUTION

In the same year that Tennyson went up to Trinity, Charles Darwin entered Christ's College. His father hoped he would become a clergyman, thinking his interest in natural history was not likely to lead to a profession. However, Cambridge had professors of Botany and of Geology and they encouraged Darwin's interests. Professor Henslow recommended Darwin for the post of naturalist on the *Beagle*, a ship setting off to survey South America and the Pacific. Thus Darwin began the work that resulted in *The Origin of Species*.

By the time Darwin's own sons had grown up, Cambridge was teaching and examining degree courses in the sciences. George, Horace and Francis Darwin all studied at Trinity and remained in Cambridge. They were of the generation that was at last allowed to marry without relinquishing fellowships, and they all brought up their families in Cambridge. In time, George's son Charles became Master of Christ's, his grandfather's college.

THE CAVENDISH LABORATORY

The decision in the early 1870s to set up a degree course in experimental physics was hotly debated, but the point was won by the progressives and the University's Chancellor, the Duke of Devonshire (whose family name was Cavendish), paid for the laboratory. After 1874 when the Cavendish Laboratory was completed, physicists became some of the University's most famous members. They included students who had graduated at other universities, such as Ernest Rutherford from New Zealand. He came to the Laboratory in 1895 to work under J J Thomson on electromagnetic waves, and in 1908 won the Nobel Prize for Chemistry. After several years spent teaching in other universities, he returned to Cambridge as Cavendish Professor in 1919, and during the 1920s and 1930s headed research into the splitting of the atom and the behaviour of its components.

Other Cambridge Nobel Prize winners include father and son W H and W L Bragg who studied X-rays and crystal structures and won the Physics Prize in 1915, and E D Adrian who won the Physiology and Medicine Prize in 1932. Francis Crick and James Watson (together with Maurice Wilkins) won the Physiology and Medicine Prize in 1962 for their work on the structure of DNA, the

genetic code which determines heredity, and Sir Nevill Mott who was Cavendish Professor between 1954 and 1971 was one of the joint winners of the Physics Prize in 1977.

CAMBRIDGE TO BLOOMSBURY

Several young men who were to form a lasting association, known to the outside world as the Bloomsbury Group, arrived at Trinity in 1899. The original nucleus was the Stephens family, of which the brothers Thoby and Adrian went to Trinity. There they met Leonard Woolf, who was later to marry their sister Virginia, and Clive Bell who married sister Vanessa. Also at Trinity was Lytton Strachey. Woolf and Strachey became members of the Apostles, and went to assess the qualities of another prospective member, Maynard Keynes. He, like the younger Darwins, was Cambridge born. His father was a Fellow of Pembroke and his mother became a Mayor of Cambridge. Keynes entered public life as an economist at the Peace Conference after World War I.

Grantchester, with the overshadowed river, the bees and their honey in his landlord's garden and the silent church clock. At King's College he enjoyed a range of student activities, political, dramatic and literary, and he was elected an Apostle. After graduating he lodged in Grantchester, first at the Orchard then at the Old Vicarage, while working for a fellowship. He was an attractive but sometimes unconventional figure who shocked the worthies of Grantchester by appearing in public view barefoot. His death early in World War I epitomised the loss of a generation of promising young men. His name is inscribed with the war dead on the village memorial and in King's College Chapel.

THE FOOTLIGHTS

Since the revival of amateur dramatics amongst the students about a century ago, Cambridge has produced a succession of performers known through stage, screen, radio and television. Jack and Claude Hulbert were members of the Footlights Dramatic Club in the 1910s, Richard Murdoch in 1925 and Jimmy Edwards in 1939. Club members in the 1920s included Norman Hartnell and Cecil Beaton, whose talents for design were used in the Club's productions. Another drama group, The Mummers, was founded in 1929 by Alastair Cook, writer of the *Letters from America*. However, he was less successful at talent-spotting, for he told James Mason, then at Magdalene College, to stick to architecture. In the 1950s and 1960s Cambridge (and Oxford) graduates led new movements in entertainment and humour, and Jonathan Miller, Peter Cook, David Frost, Eleanor Bron and many, many others became known to everyone with a television set.

AS WAR BEGAN
Rupert Brooke, who had rooms in King's College Fellows' Building before he moved out to Grantchester, was instrumental in founding the Marlowe Society for undergraduate dramatics

'GRANTCHESTER, AH GRANTCHESTER'

Keynes' brother Geoffrey became a close friend of another King's student, Rupert Brooke. Brooke's name is, for most people, linked with Grantchester, a village two miles from Cambridge (see page 76). Like many students he had no sympathy with Cambridge town, and in the poem *The Old Vicarage, Grantchester* wrote:

For Cambridge people rarely smile,
Being urban, squat and packed with guile

However, he loved the 'holy quiet' of

ROYAL PERFORMANCE
Prince Edward, during his time at Cambridge, enjoyed acting. He is seen here in a production of The Taming of the Shrew

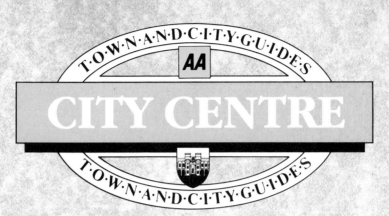

CITY CENTRE

Bicycles—readily available for hire—are one of the best ways of negotiating the city's alleyways and narrow, busy streets

ABBEY HOUSE/BARNWELL PRIORY

Abbey Road (off Newmarket Road)
Abbey House occupies part of the site of the old Augustinian Barnwell Priory which was dissolved in 1538. All that remains of the priory is a vaulted chamber known as the Cellarer's Chequer (which may have been part of the kitchen) at the corner of Beche and Priory Roads, and the nearby small 13th-century church of St Andrew the Less which was attached to the priory. By the end of the 16th century stone from

An entrance to Abbey House

the priory was being removed for buildings elsewhere; some was used in the construction of Corpus Christi Chapel.

The house itself, which is privately occupied, is a mixture of timber-framed and brick construction, built in three phases between the late 16th and 18th centuries. On the attractive 'Dutch' west gable, with its altered windows, the date 1678 can be seen.

ADDENBROOKE'S HOSPITAL

Trumpington Street
The old hospital, opposite the Fitzwilliam Museum, was founded and endowed in the 18th century by Dr John Addenbrooke, a Fellow of St Catharine's College. It was reconstructed by Sir Matthew Digby Wyatt in 1863–4, and fragments of the original building were incorporated in the structure. An ugly top storey was later added to the façade.

By the mid 20th century new buildings were urgently needed, and the New Addenbrooke's Hospital

was developed on a site to the south of the city. The first buildings were opened by the Queen in 1962. Since then New Addenbrooke's has become a regional hospital and medical school and maintains close connections with the University.

The University bought the site of the Old Hospital in 1986, after it had closed, and proposed to pull the building down. However, local opposition has been considerable and as a result the façade at least may be preserved.

ALL SAINTS CHURCH

Jesus Lane
This is one of several disused churches in Cambridge now in the care of the Redundant Churches Fund. It was built in the mid-1860s in Gothic Revival style by George Bodley. William Morris was commissioned to decorate the interior walls and ceilings. In addition there are Minton tiles in the chancel, and the east window has figures designed by the young Burne-Jones, by Ford Madox Brown and by Morris.

BARNWELL PRIORY

See Abbey House

BOTANIC GARDEN

The original University Botanic Garden, founded in 1762 by Dr Richard Walker, Vice-Master of Trinity College, was used mainly for the study of medicinal plants. It was sited on five acres of land off Free School Lane, later to be built over to form the New Museums Site.

Although land for a new garden in the south of the town was purchased in 1831, it was another 15 years before the gardens were officially opened. A plaque on the large lime tree near the Trumpington Road entrance commemorates the date, 9 November 1846. The new 40-acre site, bordered by Hills Road, Bateman Street and Trumpington Road, was not all developed immediately, but early features include most of the large trees, the systematic beds with the plants grouped according to their botanical relationships, the lake and rock garden, and the glasshouses. The eastern half of the garden site was used as allotments until after World War II, when the bequest left by Reginald Cory enabled the more recent features to be developed.

Today the attractions include the chronological bed, planted according to the date of introduction of the plants, the scented garden, and the conservation garden which contains species rare in their natural habitat in Britain.

BRIDGES

During its passage through Cambridge the River Cam is crossed by a railway, five public highways, eight public footbridges, and six private college bridges. It was first bridged, before 875, near Magdalene College; the present 1823 bridge, strengthened in the 1970s, is an unusual three-pin cast-iron arch. Silver Street has had one or more bridges since the 14th century— indeed, at one time, the road was known as Small Bridges Street. The newer bridges are further out from the city centre. Fen Causeway was built in 1924–8 to provide work for the unemployed, and Elizabeth Way Bridge in 1971 to take pressure off the 1890 iron Victoria Avenue Bridge to its west.

The oldest surviving college bridge, Clare Bridge (1638–40), is much more graceful than James Essex's Trinity Bridge (1764–5), to its north, or William Wilkins' King's Bridge (1819), to its south.

The original wooden Queens' Bridge (now known as the 'Mathematical Bridge') designed by undergraduate W Etheridge, was completed in 1750. The myth that it was constructed by interlocking straight pieces of timber in such a

Stained-glass in All Saints Church

The lake and glasshouses at the University Botanic Garden

The Garden's chronological bed

way that no nails or bolts were necessary is probably untrue. The present copy, dating from 1902, does have bolts, and resulted in another myth that students were used to take the earlier bridge to pieces but were unable (or too inebriated) to put it back together again. The northernmost college bridges belong to St John's: the covered bridge by Henry Hutchinson, which resembles the Venetian 'Bridge of Sighs', built in 1831 to connect the older courts with New Court, and Sir Christopher Wren's attractive bridge of 1709–12 (known as the Kitchen Bridge or Old Bridge) a few yards to the south.

Since the 16th century there has been a public right of way over the Backs by successive Garret Hostel bridges, the present one being constructed in 1960. All the other public footbridges date from the late 19th or 20th centuries.

CAIUS COLLEGE

See Gonville and Caius College

CAMBRIDGE CASTLE

Castle Street
All that remains of the Norman castle which once dominated Cambridge is an earth mound in the grounds of the modern Shire Hall. However, it is worth climbing the mound on a fine day for the excellent view of Cambridge it affords. The castle, built for William the Conqueror in the early days of his reign, was a wooden motte and bailey construction. In the 13th century it was rebuilt in stone by Edward I, but by the 16th century it had fallen into disrepair. Queen Mary I is said to have granted some of the stone from the castle to the Huddleston family of Sawston Hall

who had sheltered her in 1553 (as she fled from Lady Jane Grey's supporters), and whose hall had, as a result, been burnt by local Protestants.

CHRIST'S COLLEGE

St Andrew's Street
This college is attractive in itself and interesting for its associations, with John Milton (see page 28), Charles Darwin (see page 30) and Field-Marshal Smuts (the Afrikaner soldier-statesman) among its more famous graduates. The college, founded in the 1440s on the site of what is now King's College Chapel, was originally known as God's House. However, when Henry VI wanted the land for his own King's College, it was moved to its present position. In 1505 Lady Margaret Beaufort (mother of Henry VII) renamed it Christ's College. She also provided funds for a college nurse, a country shelter from plague, and clean surplices. Lady Margaret's arms, over the main gate, are similar to those over the gate of her other college, St John's.

The First Court of Christ's College was completed in 1511, incorporating in the gatehouse wing earlier buildings of God's House. Originally of clunch and red brick, the façades were re-faced in stone during the 18th century. The hall was altered and panelled by James Essex in the mid 18th century and later (between 1876 and 1879) was entirely rebuilt, using the old materials, by George Gilbert Scott. There are many early features in the chapel and notable stained-glass in its north windows, some of which may have come from the old God's House. The east window of 1912 is thought to depict Henry VII as well

as Lady Margaret Beaufort and John Fisher (her Confessor), with the college itself in the background.

A very attractive Fellows' Building was added in the 1640s on the far side of Second Court. Behind the building is the Fellows' Garden with its 17th-century college 'Bath' and 18th-century summer-house. Also in the garden is Milton's mulberry tree. Sometimes said to have been planted by the poet, it is more likely to be one of 300 mulberries introduced by the college in 1608 (coincidentally the year of Milton's birth) for James I, who was keen to produce English silk.

At the far northern side of the college site, backing onto King Street, is an architecturally interesting, pyramid-like building designed by Denys Lasdun.

CHURCHILL COLLEGE

Storey's Way
This national memorial to Sir Winston Churchill, founded in the early 1960s, was intended particularly for students studying engineering, mathematics and the natural sciences—a visit by Churchill to Massachusetts Institute of Technology led to a wish to encourage this area of education. It has flats for married students and was the first college in which senior members sat in the dining hall together with junior members instead of on a raised dais (or 'High Table') at one end.

The college buildings consist of a series of three-storey open blocks, designed by Richard Sheppard, and built mainly of stone-coloured bricks and slabs of concrete patterned by wood shuttering. Between the buildings are modern sculptures by artists such as Henry Moore and Barbara Hepworth.

General de Gaulle gave the college a Jean Lurçat tapestry which is displayed in the library named after Brendan Bracken, a faithful political friend of Sir Winston.

CLARE COLLEGE

Trinity Lane

This was the first college in which undergraduates and Fellows lived together as a community—the idea of the effective foundress, Lady Elizabeth de Clare who, in 1338, took over the earlier University Hall and re-endowed it. A fire in 1521 led to rebuilding between 1523 and 1535. However, by the early 17th century the buildings were in disrepair and the college was almost completely rebuilt in the 17th and 18th centuries.

There are two distinct parts to the college, which is divided by Queen's Road. The Old Court off Trinity Lane is very much of one style, although the building of it was delayed by the Civil War of the 1640s and took 130 years (1638–1769). The early buildings include the chapel, which extends outside the court towards the lane and has an altar-piece by Cipriani. A footpath, past Clare's gardens and over the lovely 17th-century bridge, leads to Memorial Court, designed by Sir Giles Gilbert Scott in memory of the members of Clare who were killed in World War I. The new library, opened in 1986, was built in the middle of this court.

Among the roll-call of college Fellows have been Bishop Latimer, martyred in Mary I's reign, and Nicholas Ferrar, founder of the Little Gidding religious community in Huntingdonshire—which devoted itself to prayer and fine bookbinding. Famous undergraduates of the college include Charles Marquess Cornwallis, who surrendered to the rebellious North American colonists at Yorktown in 1781.

CORN EXCHANGE, THE

Wheeler Street

The Corn Exchange, behind the Guildhall, and across the street from the Tourist Information Centre, was built in 1874 from local brick and iron roof ribs shipped from Antwerp. Its name explains its original use; it once housed about 130 stands where the county's farmers could trade their produce. When, in the 1950s, it was no longer needed for this purpose, it served for many years as a public hall, being used for roller-skating, dances, beer festivals and other events. It was renovated in the early 1980s and at the end of 1986 was re-opened as a modern 1,450-seat concert hall with excellent acoustics. The cleaned brickwork reveals colours and shapes of surprising variety. The building's origins are indicated by the stone panels either side of the main entrance as well as in the frieze of farming activities inside.

CORPUS CHRISTI COLLEGE

Trumpington Street

Originally known as Bene't College, and standing between the churches of St Bene't and St Botolph, Corpus is unique among Cambridge colleges in that it was founded, in 1352, by two town guilds rather than by a monarch or other rich benefactor. Old Court, a lovely 14th-century enclosed court and the earliest surviving in Cambridge, is at the northern, Bene't Street end of the college. The buildings are linked by a gallery to St Bene't's Church, which served as the college chapel until 1579.

New Court or Second Court, of 1823–7, is joined to Old Court by a passage-way in the middle of the south range of buildings which contains the hall. William Wilkins designed New Court in the Gothic Revival style, a remarkable contrast with his earlier Downing College buildings. Wilkins' chapel, on the east side, replaced an earlier one on the same site which had been built in the 16th century largely at the expense of Sir Nicholas Bacon, father of Francis Bacon and a Corpus graduate. Queen Elizabeth I and Sir Francis Drake also contributed to the costs of this earlier chapel. The library, on the south side of the court, contains a priceless collection of manuscripts and early printed books salvaged at the Dissolution of the Monasteries by Matthew Parker, Master of the college between 1544 and 1553 and later Archbishop of Canterbury. Parker is commemorated by a statue outside the chapel, and also commemorated, by a plaque, is the Elizabethan dramatist Christopher Marlowe who was a student at the college.

Old Court, Corpus Christi College

DARWIN COLLEGE

Silver Street

Darwin College, which consists of a line of houses between the street and the River Cam, joined together to make a terrace, does not immediately look like a Cambridge college. The modern architecture linking the old houses can be clearly seen from Silver Street; the picturesque river side is best viewed from the end of Mill Lane. In the centre of the range is Newnham Grange, joined to a little island by a bridge. The Grange was, from 1885, the home of George Darwin, son of Charles Darwin, famous author of *The Origin of Species*. Darwin College was founded in 1964 to cater for research students and senior University members who otherwise had no effective college links.

DOWNING COLLEGE

Regent Street

The view into the college from the entrance off Regent Street is all space, light and proportion. A grass area, larger even than Trinity's Great Court, is flanked by stone buildings on only three sides. The neo-Grecian style seems appropriate for an institution intentionally different in many ways from the older colleges. It was the first new foundation since the 16th century, and later had the first married Fellows, as well as the first endowed professorships in Law and Mathematics.

William Wilkins, at the age of 24, won a competition to design the new college. His plan was to space out the college buildings instead of making enclosed courts, thus effectively creating the first campus—10 years before Jefferson built the University of Virginia campus at Charlottesville. The endowment for the college came from Sir George Downing, who died in 1749, but building was long delayed by a bitter and costly lawsuit

over his will—so costly that money ran short before building was completed. The east and west ranges, in classical style, were built between 1807 and 1821 and more was added in 1874–6, following Wilkins' plans. His intention was to have a large entrance gate in the northern area, but when building was finally resumed in the 1930s and 1950s this was completely filled in.

DOWNING STREET SITES

On either side of Downing Street are crowded a number of different scientific departments which have always been enormously important in the development of the sciences. Included in the site, with its entrance on Free School Lane, is the Whipple Museum of the History of Science (see page 53).

The northern New Museums Site was developed in the 19th century in an area once occupied by an Augustinian friary, Cambridge's first secondary school—the Perse—and the original 18th-century Botanic Garden. The site was named after the 'new' Museum of Anatomy, opened in 1833. For the last 150 years the area has been crammed tighter and tighter with buildings serving ever-changing scientific purposes. The Cavendish Laboratory of 1874, creation of William Cavendish, Duke of Devonshire and Chancellor of the University, was world famous for the fundamental physics investigated there (see page 31). Great scientific achievements were also made in other departments on the New Museums Site; an example is the work of the biochemist Sir Frederick Gowland Hopkins who 'discovered' vitamins.

After World War II the Cavendish Laboratory moved into a new building west of Cambridge off the Madingley Road, an area envisaged as a future science campus, and the Chemistry Laboratory, too, moved out to Lensfield Road. But many of the science departments are still based on the New Museums Site, with new departments, such as aerial photography, computing, and audio-visual aids, taking the place of the older ones.

The 'Downing' site to the south of Downing Street was acquired by the University between 1896 and 1902 and filled with new scientific buildings, some departments moving from the older New Museums Site. The buildings facing Downing Street currently house the Department of Earth Sciences and

the Faculty of Archaeology and Anthropology, both of which have fascinating museums (see page 50 and page 44).

One of the carved prehistoric animals on the Downing Street buildings

EAGLE, THE

Bene't Street
This old coaching inn, originally named the Eagle and Child, is entered through an archway from Bene't Street. The courtyard is noteworthy for its first-floor open gallery, dating from around 1800, which is attached to the oldest part of the inn, built some 200 years before. The inn has long been a favourite haunt of students and it was here that many of Crick and Watson's discussions on DNA (see page 31) took place.

EMMANUEL COLLEGE

St Andrew's Street
Built on the site of a Dominican friary, and founded in the 1580s by a leading Elizabethan Puritan, Sir Walter Mildmay, Emmanuel has particular associations for Americans. Out of 100 Cambridge graduates who emigrated to New England before 1646, 35 came from Emmanuel, among them John Harvard who gave his name and his library to the American university. His life is commemorated by a plaque in the chapel.

Front Court together with the inappropriately named New Court was the core of the original college, lying between Emmanuel and St Andrew's Streets. Only the west and east ranges of New Court and the

range which divides it from Front Court now remain from the buildings of the 1580s. The old courts include the friary church, transformed into the College Hall and refitted in the late 18th century by the Cambridge architect James Essex Junior who also re-faced the south front of this hall range in ashlar and built the heavy, west entrance front.

On entering the college from St Andrew's Street through Essex's range, the building opposite is Sir Christopher Wren's Chapel and Cloister (dating from the 1660s) and, on the right, is the Westmorland Building—largely financed by the 6th Earl of Westmorland and designed by a committee. It was built midway in time between Wren's chapel and Essex's front.

Emmanuel College is fortunate in the space which it has available and is well known for its attractive gardens. Around the lawns and lakes of the Paddock and Chapman's Garden are grouped the college's more modern buildings.

FESTIVAL THEATRE

Newmarket Road
A plain building on the opposite side of the road to the *Cambridge Evening News* office houses a small theatre built in 1814 and originally known as the Theatre Royal. In the 1860s it became a Mission Hall but then was re-opened as the Festival Theatre between the wars. Many future famous actors and actresses including Robert Donat and Flora Robson made their debut here. Despite being closed again in 1934 it still retains most of its early 19th-century interior arrangements although the seating has been removed. Today it is used as a store by its successor, the Arts Theatre, which was founded in 1936.

FITZWILLIAM COLLEGE

Huntingdon Road
Fitzwilliam College began in 1869 as a non-collegiate community founded for men who wished to study but did not want to, or could not afford to, belong to a college. Its first home was a Georgian house opposite the Fitzwilliam Museum in Trumpington Street. In the 1960s Fitzwilliam became a full college and moved into buildings designed by the architect Denys Lasdun. The glass and concrete vault of the present dining hall is particularly striking, as is the college's new block on Storey's Way.

FITZWILLIAM MUSEUM

Trumpington Street
The Fitzwilliam is one of the oldest
and most remarkable museums in
the country, containing some of the
best collections of ceramics,
paintings, coins, medals and
antiquities outside London. Its
collections are housed in an
imposing temple designed
specifically for the purpose by
George Basevi in 1834. The
museum was eventually opened in
1848, and there have been
subsequent additions, the most
recent in 1975, when the restaurant
and shop were added.

The museum's founder, Richard
7th Viscount Fitzwilliam of
Merrion, bequeathed 144 paintings
to the University in 1816, along with
books, prints and 130 illuminated
manuscripts. His portrait as a
Cambridge undergraduate in 1764,
by Joseph Wright of Derby, hangs
in the room at the top of the stairs.

Under the fine Corinthian portico
is excellent bold early Victorian
plasterwork. The entrance hall, one
of the finest of any provincial
museum, has the grandeur of a
London club, and, indeed, it is the
work of Sir Charles Barry, architect
of the Reform Club in London.
Perhaps he wanted to give an
appropriately exclusive air to the
museum; when it was first opened it
was only available to the 'properly
dressed' public on three days of the
week. Even members of the
University, who could use it at other
times of the week, had to be dressed
'in Academical Habit'.

In the **Lower Galleries** are
antiquities, ceramics, coins and
medals, and armour. At the bottom

The Indiscreet Harlequin—*English
porcelain from the Bow Factory—dates
from the 1750s. It is a copy of a Meissen
figure group*

*The opulent entrance hall of the museum,
with its twin staircases, statues and
marble columns, was designed by Sir
Charles Barry*

of the right-hand stairs the Egyptian
antiquities rooms contain coffin
cases showing the journey of
Espawershefi through the
Netherworld, protected by the
Goddess Nut. Also on display is a
rare collection of Egyptian drawings
on flakes of limestone. The rooms to
the left contain Greek and Roman
antiquities: for example, the Roman
mosaic fountain niche, and part of a
Roman couch, painstakingly
restored from fragments by
members of the museum's staff.
These rooms also contain the
magnificent Bacchanalian
procession of the Pashley
Sarcophagus (*c.*AD130).

Glass doors lead to the English
and Continental ceramics galleries,
the Fisher and Glaisher
collections—the latter without
doubt the best collection of ceramics
outside London. Exhibits range
from 17th-century
English brown-glazed earthenware
to fine chinoiserie Meissen, red
anchor Chelsea and Victorian Parian
figures. The Far Eastern gallery is at
the right-hand end of the second
pottery gallery: a Ming dynasty
buffalo in green jade, until 1900 part
of the furnishings of the Winter
Palace in Peking and now one of the

largest pieces of jade sculpture in
Western collections, is one of the
highlights here. The room also
contains 11th-century Sung dynasty
porcelain, as well as later enamelled
18th-century porcelain, some of
which was made for export to
Europe.

At the other end of the pottery
gallery is the armour room, with a
German fluted set for both horse
and rider, and a fine 16th-century
Milanese parade helmet in the form
of a lion mask. Two little rooms
open off the armour room. That on
the left contains coins and medals,
including Quentin Matsy's romantic
Erasmus of 1519. It also contains one
of the best small collections of
English glass in the country, much
from local sources. Arranged in
chronological order, running
clockwise from the right as you
enter, it includes a rare Elizabethan
Venetian-style soda glass, probably
by Verzelini. The room to the right
has medieval illuminated
manuscripts, including the Grey
Fitzpayn *Book of Hours*, fine Coptic
and Byzantine ivories, Gothic
carvings, and Elizabethan portrait
miniatures, including works by
Nicholas Hilliard and Isaac Oliver.

The **Upper Galleries**, devoted
primarily to paintings, were laid out
in comfortable carpeted and
furnished 'state room' manner by
Sidney Cockerell, Director of the
Museum between 1908 and 1937. He

is said to have remarked, 'I found it a pig stye, I turned it into a palace'. The Early Italian Renaissance paintings are reached through the French Impressionist room to the left of the main stairs. Of late 15th-century date is a fine cassone panel, from a marriage chest, appropriately decorated by Jacopo del Sellaio with part of the Story of Cupid and Psyche, composed almost in cartoon-strip style; across the room is a painting of the *Virgin with Saints* by Cosimo Rosselli. On a small wall nearby the delightful Florentine perspective setting of Domenico Veneziano's *Annunciation* can be seen.

Treasures of the later Italian Renaissance in the room beyond include the landscape of *Castel Gandolfo* by Claude Lorraine; the minute, mysterious Elsheimer of *Minerva and Venus*, painted on copper; Titian's *Rape of Lucretia* and *Venus and a Lute-player*; and Veronese's *Hermes, Herse, and Aglauros*. At the far end of this large Italian room, past Canaletto's works, is the Flemish room with Joos van Cleve's good-humoured

Claude Monet's Le Printemps, *painted in 1886, numbers among the museum's rich collection of French Impressionist paintings*

The Messel-Rosse Feather Fan probably came from South or Central America

Virgin and Child, sketches by Rubens, early Flemish landscapes, and Spanish paintings by Murillo and others. Back through the large room an often unfairly ignored collection of Dutch 17th-century flower paintings is reached. The Dutch paintings room beyond has almost a history of Dutch landscapes from Van Goyen's low viewpoint to Philips de Koninck's panorama, and good small genre scenes by Jan Steen and Gerard Dou, a pupil of Rembrandt.

Through a small lecture theatre,

and the Adeane gallery which houses temporary exhibitions, is the 20th-century gallery, containing works ranging from Graham Sutherland's *Crucifixion* to Kitaj's *Thanksgiving*.

Returning to the top of the main stairs the French Impressionist gallery is reached. This contains Renoir's *Gust of Wind*, Monet's *Le Printemps*, Pissarro's *Garden at Pontoise*, and Degas' moving *Au Café*. In the next room French paintings of the 17th to 19th centuries can be seen: from Poussin's *Rebecca and Eliezer at the Well*, to Fabre's *Allen Smith Contemplating the Arno*, and Courbet's fresh green *La Ronde Enfantine*.

To the right in the large room of 16th- to 18th-century paintings are excellent portraits by Van Dyck, Hogarth, Gainsborough, Reynolds and Raeburn, as well as Stubbs' *Gimcrack*, a recent purchase. The 19th-century English room beyond contains Constable's *Hampstead Heath*, and Millais' startling gold and blue *Bridesmaid*. The next room is the early 20th-century paintings gallery with works by Sickert, Gilman and Gore influenced by Impressionism, and French works ranging from the sober structures of Cubism to the fresh colour of Matisse.

The 16th-century building housing the Cambridge and County Folk Museum seen from across Castle Street

FOLK MUSEUM

Castle Street
The museum, opened in 1936, is housed in the former White Horse Inn—a 16th-century timber-framed building which has been altered and extended over the years. Its interior, with narrow stairs and well-worn creaky wooden floors is singularly appropriate as a setting for the numerous bygones collected over the last three centuries from Cambridge and the surrounding area.

The exhibits are fascinating and wide-ranging, and those relating to children and their toys are especially popular.

Other items of particular interest are arranged as follows, starting with tools and implements of local trades in the first ground-floor room. In the second room, the inn's original bar, cooking and lighting equipment can be seen; there are also cigarette boxes, tea caddies, jelly moulds and sugar-loaf cutters. The third room has cooking and washing equipment, an amazing early refrigerator and vacuum cleaners. Upstairs samplers and similar handicrafts decorate one room, whilst the next has a wonderful variety of objects ranging from Aldermen's gowns to inn signs, and from a broadsheet of the execution of two murderers to a drawing of an 1877 local aerial machine which actually flew! Then come the children's rooms. The third floor contains a collection of fenlanders' tools.

GIRTON COLLEGE

Huntingdon Road
Girton, the first women's college in either Oxford or Cambridge, originated in the movement to gain higher education for women. In 1869 Emily Davies, together with friends, rented Benslow House in Hitchin, 26 miles from Cambridge, and persuaded a few Cambridge

lecturers to travel to Hitchin to teach the five women students. Hitchin had been chosen because it kept the female students well away from the male undergraduates, but when the Benslow House lease ended in 1872 it was decided to move nearer to Cambridge, and Girton, 2½ miles from the town centre, was chosen—still a safe distance from temptation.

The initial college consisted of only one wing and a small hall, but as the number of students grew other buildings by Waterhouse and his son were added. Its remoteness has compensations; no other college has so much open space and garden around it—nearly 50 acres in all.

By 1881 women were allowed to attend University lectures and take examinations, but it was not until 1948—after much hostility—that the first woman graduate at Cambridge was awarded a degree.

As well as being the first Oxbridge women's college, Girton can also claim other firsts. It was the first college to have rooms opening off corridors not off separate staircases, and the first women's college to admit men.

Red-brick flying buttresses at Girton College which opened in 1873

GONVILLE AND CAIUS COLLEGE

Trinity Street and Senate House Passage
The college's name commemorates its two founders. The first of these, Edmund Gonville, was responsible for the hall which was built around Gonville Court after 1353. Behind the 18th-century ashlar façades of this court many of the 14th- and 15th-century buildings still exist. John Keys, latinised to Caius (but

still pronounced Keys), re-founded the college in 1557 and became Master in 1559. He built Caius Court with its south side open, 'lest the air from being confined within a narrow space should become foul, and so do harm to us, and still more to Gonville's College'. Caius was also responsible for one of the jewels of the college, the Gate of Honour which links Caius Court and Senate House Passage. This is the third of Dr Caius' gates which are remarkable for their early (1565–75) use of classical details. The new student entered through the Gate of Humility, rebuilt in the Master's garden, passed through Virtue (still the entrance to Caius Court) to his lodging, and out through Honour to his graduation.

The chapel, between Gonville and Caius Courts, dates originally from the 14th century though it has been altered and extended over the years. It contains three remarkable tombs high up on its walls, those of Thomas Legge—Master of the college in the early 17th century, of Stephen Perse—founder of the Perse School, and of Dr Caius.

From Trinity Street and King's Parade the most obvious part of Caius (the abbreviated name by which the college is usually known) is Alfred Waterhouse's 19th-century building around Tree Court.

Caius College has always had strong links with the medical sciences, Caius himself being a Norfolk physician who had studied at Europe's leading medical school of the time, Padua, as well as at Gonville Hall. In his will Dr Caius provided for the cleaning of pavements and gutters inside and outside the college. A little later, at the end of the 16th century, William

Harvey, who discovered the circulation of blood, graduated from the college.

Gonville and Caius' Gate of Honour

GREAT ST ANDREW'S CHURCH

St Andrew's Street
Great St Andrew's, or St Andrew the Great Church, is no longer used as a place of worship, but its eye-catching position opposite Christ's College has made its future a centre of controversy. In 1842 the church was completely rebuilt, by subscription, in late 15th-century Gothic style. Because it contains many memorials, including one to Captain James Cook, the current proposal to turn it into shops is bitterly opposed.

GREAT ST MARY'S CHURCH

King's Parade
St Mary the Great Church, known after 1352 as Gt St Mary's, and commonly called the University Church, used to be the administrative and ceremonial centre of the University, and distances from Cambridge are measured from here. It has undergone two major rebuildings: the first followed a fire in 1290 (parts of the chancel walls are all that remain of this); the second began in 1478, most of the building being completed by 1514. The tower, however, was not finished until nearly 100 years later when Robert Grumbold added the corner turrets. It is well worth climbing the tower for the view of the city it provides.

St Mary's Late Perpendicular style of building is seen at its best from the inside. The roof, the original timbers for which were given by Henry VII, was repaired and preserved by the elder James Essex in 1726. As the University Church, Great St Mary's has hosted many famous preachers and pressure for more seating accommodation led to the building of the galleries in the 18th century.

An unusual feature of the church is the pulpit which runs on brass rails and can be moved from one side of the chancel to the other.

GUILDHALL

Market Hill
This building, on the south side of the Market Square, is where the locally elected council which governs the city is based. The present Guildhall was built in 1938–9 and contains two halls used for public functions, the Council Chamber, and working offices. Incorporated into the back of the building, facing Wheeler Street, are parts of the older Guildhall built between 1859 and 1895, and now housing the Tourist Information Centre.

HOBSON'S CONDUIT

Junction of Lensfield Road and Trumpington Road
This fountain, resembling a pepper-pot topped by a fir-cone, was erected in the Market Square in 1614 and moved to its present position in 1856. Water was brought in from Shelford, south of Cambridge, and distributed at the conduit-head; open gutters which used to flow with this water can still be seen in some streets such as Trumpington Street.

The conduit was named after Thomas Hobson (1544–1630), the Cambridge carrier who was its chief

benefactor. This is the same Hobson who has become immortalised in the phrase 'Hobson's Choice', based on his practice of insisting that hirers took the horse nearest the door. This enforced rotation of horses prevented everyone choosing, and thus overworking, his best animals.

HOLY SEPULCHRE CHURCH

See Round Church

HOLY TRINITY CHURCH

Market Street
Holy Trinity Church, on the corner of Market and Sidney Streets, is notable for its associations with the evangelical revival. Charles Simeon, Fellow of King's College and evangelical divine, became vicar in the 1780s; his style of preaching was carried on after his death in 1836. Simeon's memorial tablet is in the chancel. In the chancel there is also a memorial to the Reverend Henry Martyn who translated the New Testament into Hindustani and Persian. It is thought that Simeon's influence led to his decision to sail for India in 1805 to work as a missionary.

The church itself dates mainly from the 14th and 15th centuries, but has a 19th-century chancel. The 15th-century wooden roofs of the nave and transepts spring from stone corbels with angels. Early in the 17th century galleries were put up to accommodate the audience for a 'town lectureship'; only one gallery, in the south transept, remains.

The decorative top of Hobson's Conduit, stone fountain of 1614

JESUS COLLEGE

Jesus Lane
A number of the buildings of Jesus College are adorned with three cock heads, the rebus or sign of Bishop John Alcock of Ely who in 1496 adapted the buildings of a suppressed nunnery, St Radegund's, for his new college. The high-walled passage-way 'The Chimney' leads from the 18th-century gateway by Robert Grumbold on Jesus Lane through the Tudor gatehouse into First or Outer Court. This, together with Cloister Court, contains the oldest buildings of the college.

The central archway in the 13th-century range on the east of Outer Court leads into Cloister Court, round which the layout and fabric of the Benedictine nunnery largely survive. Facing you as you enter Cloister Court are the fine Early English arches of the entrance to the former Chapter House. The Refectory, now the College Hall, was in the northern range, and on the south was the church. Much of the nave became the Master's Lodge, but the rest, with the crossing, the transepts and the chancel, is now the College Chapel, which is both a Gothic and a Gothic Revival monument. The chapel underwent two main periods of restoration in the 19th century. Pugin's glass and woodwork have transformed the chancel; Ford Madox Brown and Burne-Jones glass fills the nave and transept windows and the design of the crossing and nave roofs is by William Morris.

Jesus College has had several famous archbishops as members, the best known being Cranmer who compiled the English prayer book before his death as a martyr in Oxford (see page 28). Laurence Sterne, author of *Tristram Shandy* and Samuel Taylor Coleridge (see page 29) were students at the college as, recently, was Prince Edward.

KETTLE'S YARD

Northampton Street
On the northern side of Northampton Street there appears to be a village green with an old people's home, a group of cottages with a simple modern barn-like building, and St Peter's church tower in the background. But the cottages, linked together by the barn-like extension gallery, house the art collection of Jim Ede, a personal exploration of 20th-century art. Jim Ede created the external setting as well as the interior, and left his extraordinary collection,

Art at Kettle's Yard

which includes works by Henri Gaudier-Brzeska, Alfred Wallis and Ben Nicholson, to the University. The interiors are a surprisingly effective combination of domestic scale with a multi-level exhibition gallery. A separate gallery for visiting exhibitions has been added at the back.

KING'S COLLEGE

King's Parade
King's College was founded in 1441 by Henry VI as a college for the scholars from his school at Eton. His first plans were for a small college of approximately 12 scholars, but then his ideas became grander with a scheme for a college of nearly 100 people, including 70 scholars and 16 choir boys. Sites were acquired and buildings demolished to make room for this new college, but only the Old Court (later rebuilt and now part of the Old Schools) and the chapel (see page 20) were built. Henry VI's connections with the college are commemorated by a statue which surmounts the fountain in Front Court.

The other college buildings, which date from the 18th century or later, were mostly built to be stylistically in keeping with the chapel. It pinnacles and windows are echoed in William Wilkins' screen wall and gatehouse on King's Parade. This and the south range of Front Court, containing the hall with its two wooden lanterns and splendid interior, is Gothic Revival of 1824–8.

In sharp contrast to the rest of King's is Gibbs' Fellows' Building which faces the King's Parade entrance. James Gibbs, architect of the Senate House, created this impressive west range between 1724 and 1732. Anywhere else but alongside the Chapel, its monumental scale and splendid proportions would make it noteworthy.

Probably the most famous of King's 20th-century students was Lord Keynes, who improved the college's finances.

KING'S PARADE

Looking across the road from King's College one sees buildings with an appealing irregularity of height and style, shops below, living accommodation above. Between St Mary's and St Edward's Passages are 16th- and 17th-century buildings and a rare five-storey house of 1787. The rest of the Parade dates from the 18th and 19th centuries. Until the early 19th century the western side of King's Parade would have looked similar, with shops and houses reaching back as far as the screen wall of King's College which replaced them in the 1820s.

Overlooking the river, Bodley's Court at King's College was built during 1893 in a neo-Tudor style

Part of the war memorial outside Great St Mary's Church in King's Parade

LEYS SCHOOL, THE

Trumpington Road
Situated on a visually prominent site on the corner of Trumpington Road and Fen Causeway, this public school was established in the mid-1870s, as a Methodist foundation. Although it was originally open only to boys, it is now co-educational. Today's school shows a great mixture of buildings, the oldest of which, as shown on Baker's 1830 map, is the headmaster's house; other buildings are very new. The gateway and library, opened by George V in 1914, were designed by the architect Sir Aston Webb.

LION YARD

See Petty Cury

LITTLE ST MARY'S CHURCH

Trumpington Street
Originally dedicated to St Peter, the church gave its name to Peterhouse and served as the college chapel until 1632; church and college are

joined by a gallery. When the church was rebuilt in the mid 14th century it was dedicated to St Mary, and although the church's proper name is St Mary the Less it is more commonly known as Little St Mary's. The church is aisleless and there is no division between nave and chancel. A memorial tablet to Godfrey Washington, who died in 1729, carries the arms of the Washington family, stars and stripes surmounted by an eagle, which is thought to be the basis for the United States' flag.

MAGDALENE COLLEGE

Magdalene Street
Magdalene's First Court was built in the 15th and early 16th centuries for monks from the Benedictine monasteries of Crowland, Ely, Ramsey and Walden—modern replicas of whose coats of arms adorn its walls. At this time the college was known as Buckingham College, because of the patronage of the dukes of Buckingham. With the Dissolution of the Monasteries the college lost its money as well as its monks, but a few years later (in 1542) it was refounded by Sir Thomas Audley (of Audley End) who renamed it Magdalene College. He also appropriated the right to appoint the Master of this college, a right which is still held by his descendants.

Second Court, reached through the screens passage, contains the late 17th-century Pepys Building which houses Samuel Pepys' library, his bookshelves, books and diary. The hall of 1519 divides the two courts; it was re-panelled during Queen Anne's reign and her coat of arms is above the High Table. The hall has portraits of Samuel Pepys and Charles Kingsley, and the portrait of another graduate—Marshal of the RAF Lord Tedder—faces that of an

A gargoyle and crests decorating First Court of Magdalene College

Honorary Fellow—T S Eliot—by the double staircase which leads to the gallery.

Across Magdalene Street there have been 20th-century adaptations of houses and the upper floors of shops to student accommodation. Also on this side of the road are Mallory Court (built in 1925–6 and altered in 1952–6), commemorating the Everest climber, and Sir Edwin Lutyen's Benson Court.

MOUNT PLEASANT AND POUND HILL

Anyone interested in urban renewal would find a walk in this area rewarding. In the 1950s Pound Hill was described as 'a humble residential district'; the description continues '. . . the whole area has a down-at-heel aspect though, in its variety, not without quaint and picturesque vistas'. By the 1970s it was derelict, but in the 1980s it has been intelligently revitalised, its vistas renewed.

To appreciate the mixture of old and new buildings and the interplay of colour from the great variety of bricks, the following route can be taken. From Northampton Street walk up Pound Hill, along Haymarket Road, and uphill round Mount Pleasant, passing *en route* Edward's House and Storey's House built in contrasting dark red bricks. At the top of Mount Pleasant and downhill, in Shelly Row, are Storey's Almshouses in yellow brick. Covering the area between Shelly Row and Castle Street a group of modern, pinkish yellow flats with outside staircases and enclosed balconies are ranged round an open courtyard.

At the bottom of Shelly Row turn left through Castle Row and left up Castle Street. The brick and timber-framed cottages facing the Shire Hall, some plaster covered, now restored and re-opened as restaurants and shops, are the oldest buildings in the area. Turn round and continue down Castle Street to the Folk Museum.

There are other blocks of modern buildings in the area and the successful restoration and adaptation of a medley of pleasant 19th-century buildings in Pound Hill and Haymarket Road is marred only by the 1884 Mission Hall and an aggressively ugly pub.

MUSEUM OF ARCHAEOLOGY AND ANTHROPOLOGY

Downing Street
This beautifully arranged museum at the Tennis Court Road corner of the Downing Street site has coloured carpets on the ground floor which guide you round numbered, attractive display cases, through the early history of the world and Britain. The subjects covered, and some of the highlights, are as follows. Brown: the evolution of man, and his use of tools and plants. Fawn: European farmers and craftsmen. Blue (the largest section):

Britain from 4000BC to the Middle Ages, emphasising Cambridgeshire, with exhibits including Iron Age scythes and napping shears, a firedog from Barton, varied Roman artefacts, and charming medieval alabaster figurines. Light brown: technology, including a reconstruction of the Somerset Sweet Track—the oldest constructed trackway in the world. Red: Africa and Asia. Green: the Americas, with enchanting little statues of animals and humans displayed next door to black and white zigzag-patterned Pueblo pots.

MUSEUM OF CLASSICAL ARCHAEOLOGY

Sidgwick Avenue
A splendidly lit, long exhibition gallery, on the first floor of the new Department of Classics, houses a remarkable collection of over 500 plaster casts of Greek and Roman reliefs and sculptures, some

Shells in the Museum of Zoology

coloured, some bronze. They are mostly life-size or larger and are displayed for study with every cast being clearly labelled. Just a few of the casts that may be seen are early Kores, the Delphi charioteer and the Venus de Milo. A cheap guide book lists them all and also provides further information.

MUSEUM OF TECHNOLOGY

Riverside (off Newmarket Road)
When the Cheddar's Lane pumping station closed in 1968, after 73 years, enthusiasts saved the building and the steam engines from destruction and, against the odds, a museum unlike anything else in Cambridge was born. Its core is a collection of working engines including two 80 horsepower Hathorn-Davey engines with two Babcock and Wilcox water-tube boilers from 1894, and two 94 horsepower gas engines, driving centrifugal pumps, which date from 1909.

Other early machines have been added since the museum was

founded, including radio, telex and computers. There is also a separate print shop with hand presses and machines for binding, cutting, and pressing books.

MUSEUM OF ZOOLOGY

Downing Street
Housed in a modern building, the museum is reached through the arch opposite the end of Tennis Court Road. Corals and shells are displayed on the top floor, with a wall-case of exotic birds on a half-way landing, and below a populated seabird landscape and another wall-case of birds. Skeletons fill the basement floor, where the exhibits are arranged to show the development of species. A wide range of animal life is covered, making it possible to compare the relative sizes of land and sea animals and of extinct and surviving species. There is also a room devoted to displays concerning man's ancestry.

NEW HALL

Huntingdon Road
In 1954 the third women's college, New Hall, was founded. It was initially based at the Hermitage in Silver Street, but 10 years later the college moved into its new white building in the north of the city. Several architectural features distinguish New Hall from other Cambridge colleges: the spine of the building is a tunnel, open on one side to a water garden below, which leads to the porter's lodge. The most visually striking part of the college is the domed dining hall with its petal-like segments.

NEWNHAM COLLEGE

Sidgwick Avenue
Two years after the foundation of Girton, Cambridge's second college for women, Newnham, came into being. Henry Sidgwick, Fellow of Trinity College, and Miss Clough, who became Principal, opened its first building in 1871, and the college moved to its present site in 1875. Six halls, joined by corridors, were built between 1875 and 1910, all designed by Basil Champneys in a red-brick Dutch style. They face an attractive open garden.

Other buildings have been added since, the most notable being the Principal's Lodge, designed by Louis Osmond. Its plan resembles a classical villa with a central court; the sheets of patterned plate glass, running from floor to roof, were designed by Geoffrey Clarke, who also worked on Coventry Cathedral.

OBSERVATORY, THE

Madingley Road
To the west of Churchill College and well back on the north side of Madingley Road are the two domes of the University Observatory—a Doric-style building designed by John Clement Mead in 1822. The original dome in the centre is flanked by two projecting wings which contained houses for the Observer and the Deputy Observer. In 1838 the Northumberland Dome to the south-west was built at the expense of the 3rd Duke of Northumberland. The recently announced closure of the Royal Greenwich Observatory at Herstmonceux, East Sussex, and the amalgamation of its activities with those of the Cambridge Observatory will have important consequences for the study of astronomy.

OLD SCHOOLS, THE

Trinity Lane and Senate House Passage
University as opposed to college buildings came relatively late to Cambridge. However, in the confused cluster of

the Old Schools, swallowed up and disguised by later work, a 14th-century building still survives. The Old Schools has two early, enclosed courts, concealed on the northern, Senate House Passage side by C R Cockerell's Library of 1837–42. This was built to house the University Library which moved out in 1934 to make room for the Squire Law Library.

Cobble (or Pebble) Court, the eastern and older of the two courts, has on the library side the Divinity School with the old Senate House above, finished in 1400. The original east side, facing King's Parade across the Senate House lawn, was replaced between 1754 and 1758 with a classical building by Stephen Wright. Its open walk with rusticated arches and windows above makes a perfect partnership with the Senate House.

Today the ground-floor rooms of Cobble Court are used as lecture rooms for the Law Faculty, the fine upstairs rooms as meeting rooms for the University's governing bodies

and for receptions. What was the Senate House is now the Combination Room with an original timber roof and plasterwork, and William Morris' famous carpet from the house 'Clouds', on the floor.

In 1829 the Old Court of King's College was bought by the University and incorporated into the Old Schools. These buildings now house the University's administration offices.

The two domes of the Observatory off Madingley Road

OUR LADY AND THE ENGLISH MARTYRS ROMAN CATHOLIC CHURCH

Hills Road
In a commanding position at the corner of Lensfield Road and Hills Road, and with the highest spire in Cambridge, this church is one of the landmarks of the city. It was completed in 1890 in Gothic Revival style. The land was provided by the Duke of Norfolk, and Mrs Lyne-Stephens, wife of an art collector, paid for the building and endowed £5,000. Some of the features for which the church is known and remembered are its bells, the polygonal east end, and the richly carved stonework.

Pembroke College: Wren's chapel, built in the 1660s on purely classical lines and extended in the 19th century by Scott, and the coat of arms

PEMBROKE COLLEGE

Trumpington Street
The gateway, the only 14th-century college entrance remaining in place, and the range which continues round the corner into Pembroke Street are all that is left of the Countess of Pembroke's 1340s foundation. As you enter Old Court through the gateway the original chapel, now the Old Library with a fine plaster ceiling and bookcases of the 1690s, is on the left. On the right is the present chapel, built in the early 1660s by Sir Christopher Wren

for his uncle, Matthew Wren, Bishop of Ely. It was Wren's first finished building and contains rare cushions of Turkey work, a type of knotted eastern carpet. Ahead is the College Hall, an 1875 replacement by Alfred Waterhouse, and the screens passage between the hall and kitchen leads into Ivy Court—built in the 17th century. The simple regularity of the north range, each dormer window with a pediment directly over two rectangular windows, contrasts with the more complex style of the later south range, the Hitcham Building.

Past members of the college include Nicholas Ridley, the Protestant martyr, Edmund Spenser, author of *The Faerie Queen*, and William Pitt the Younger, the 18th-century politician and Prime Minister (see page 29).

PERSE SCHOOL

Hills Road
Founded in 1615 by Stephen Perse of Caius College, this school has moved twice: from Free School Lane to Hills Road (on the corner of Harvey Road), in 1890, and to its present, specially designed modern building in the centre of ample playing fields in 1960. It has been, in succession, grammar, direct grant, and independent school. A separate girls' Perse School, now in Panton Street, was opened in the late 19th century.

PETERHOUSE

Trumpington Street
Cambridge's oldest college was founded by Hugh de Balsham, Bishop of Ely in the 1280s. The Hall on the south side of Old Court was begun in 1286, but was heavily reconstructed in the 1860s, as was the neighbouring Combination Room. This was Gothic Revival work: Sir George Gilbert Scott was the architect of the Hall, and William Morris and other members of his firm were responsible for the interiors of both this and the Combination Room. The rest of Old Court is of 15th-century origin with mid 18th-century re-facing. A gallery still joins the college to the neighbouring Little St Mary's Church which the college originally used as its chapel.

First Court was laid out between 1590 and the 1630s; its notable feature is the chapel, the central building which points towards the street. It was built in the late 1620s, when Matthew Wren was Master,

Peterhouse as seen from Trumpington Street. The south range of First Court is known as the library range

by George Thompson to the design of an unknown architect. The east and west fronts of the chapel provide fascinating examples of the different ways in which classical and Gothic elements could be harmoniously combined.

PETTY CURY/LION YARD

In the past Petty Cury (or Kitchen), also known at one time as Cook's Row, was an area of cobbled alleyways, coaching inns, courtyards and stables extensively used by traders, travellers, students and locals alike. Conditions were crowded, and the yard of one of the inns, the Falcon, soon deteriorated into a slum of 300 people living with little sanitation. As people left the town centre dwellings in favour of the suburbs, the inns closed and shops took their place.

In the 1960s and 1970s there was extensive redevelopment of the south side of Petty Cury, and the Lion Yard shopping precinct, named after the largest of the coaching inns on the site, was built. A focal point of the uninspiring pedestrian precinct is the large red lion outside the Public Library—this was used as the model for the lion which stands outside Waterloo Station in London. The Public Library contains an extensive Cambridgeshire Collection of local history material and frequently has displays of old prints of the town and county.

PITT BUILDING

Trumpington Street
Edward Blore was the architect of
this last phase of an early 19th-
century group of buildings
stretching between Silver Street and
Mill Lane. A fund collected for a
London statue of William Pitt gave
its surplus for the 1831–3 frontage,
hence the name. The Pitt Building
with its impressive Tudor–Gothic
tower and façade which faces
Botolph Lane was the home of the
University Press until the late 1960s,
and examples of the work done by
the Press are displayed in the
entrance hall. Recently the buildings
on the site behind the Pitt frontage
have housed peripatetic University
departments.

QUEENS' COLLEGE

Silver Street
This most charming Cambridge
college was, not surprisingly, the
first to limit its opening to visitors.
The gateway in Queens' Lane, with
coloured roof bosses, leads into a
15th-century court with a 1642
sundial on the north range. The Hall
in the west range has interior
decoration by Bodley and Morris
and fireplace tiles by Morris and
Ford Madox Brown, with portraits
of Erasmus and Elizabeth
Woodville—Edward IV's wife. She
was one of the two foundresses; the
other was Margaret of Anjou,
Henry VI's wife. Erasmus of
Rotterdam, the Renaissance scholar
and theologian, occupied the turret
in the south-west corner of this early
court between 1511 and 1514.

Cloister Court, through the
screens passage, features a unique
combination of brick cloister
arcades with a timber-framed
gallery—the President's Lodge. The
brickwork is late 15th-century, the
gallery probably Elizabethan.
Walnut Tree and Friars' Courts,
north of the first court, have a
remarkable wealth of later
buildings, from a 17th-century
range along Queens' Lane to Sir
Basil Spence's Erasmus Building of
1959–60. This was almost the first
Cambridge college building in
'modern' style and caused great
controversy when it was built.

ROBINSON COLLEGE

Grange Road
Cambridge's newest college and the
first undergraduate college founded
for both men and women, is named
after its creator, the television and
racing millionaire David Robinson.

The college, built between 1977
and 1980 of hand-made Dorset
bricks over a concrete framework, is
often described as having a fortress-
like appearance. A ramp entrance
leads into a brick street between two
walls, a layout quite unlike any other

*Robinson College, considered to be a fine
example of modern architecture*

college court. The chapel in the
street 'wall' has a stained-glass
window by John Piper and its
doorway is an attractive example of
the decorative use of brickwork.

ROUND CHURCH

Bridge Street
The Round Church or Church of the
Holy Sepulchre, on the corner of
Bridge and Round Church Streets, is
one of Cambridge's best-known
tourist attractions. Land was
granted to members of the fraternity
of the Holy Sepulchre by the Abbot
of Ramsey early in the 12th century,
and the church with its circular nave
was built. Fifteenth-century
alterations included the addition of a
polygonal belfry, but this was
destroyed during the 1841
restoration undertaken by Anthony
Salvin for the Cambridge Camden
Society. The members of this
Cambridge-based society were
devoted to the 'correct' restoration
of churches and were determined to
reinstate the original features.
Consequently, what remains now is
a wholly Norman church, albeit
heavily restored. Most of the
rectangular eastern additions date
from 1841–3 except for parts of the
chancel and its roof which are of
15th-century origin.

ST ANDREW THE GREAT CHURCH

See Great St Andrew's Church

ST BENE'T'S CHURCH

Bene't Street
St Bene't's, the oldest church in Cambridge, was built well before the Norman Conquest and the original Saxon features can be seen in the 'long and short' stonework at the corners of the tower, in the pairs of round-headed windows in the top storey of the tower, and in the tower arch inside the church featuring two carved lions. Two aisles were added to the Saxon church in the 14th century, and were later widened.

In about 1500 Dr Cosyn, Master of Corpus Christi College (formerly Bene't's College), joined the college and church by building a gallery which runs over the gateway in Free School Lane. Bene't is an abbreviation of Benedict; the apostrophe in the church's name is to indicate this.

St Bene't's has connections with several well-known Cambridge citizens. It was the burial place of Thomas Hobson the 17th-century carrier and the church also has a Bible presented by him. Later in the 17th century the clerk of St Bene't's, a man named Fabian Stedman, invented the system of change-ringing, still used by bell-ringers today.

ST BOTOLPH'S CHURCH

Trumpington Street
The dedication of this church to the fenland saint of travellers, Botolph, suggests evidence of an early church, but the oldest surviving parts, the nave and aisles, only go back to the 14th century. The

church was built near Trumpington Gate, where the road from London entered the medieval town, and travellers prayed here for a safe journey and also gave thanks when they returned safely home.

St Botolph's Church has some interesting features, especially an eye-catching Laudian font and cover. An octagonal structure in the churchyard is probably a well covering. The churchyard also contains memorials to two people responsible for much rebuilding and restoration in Cambridge: the tomb of James Essex and a memorial tablet to the mason Robert Grumbold who died in 1720.

ST CATHARINE'S COLLEGE

Trumpington Street
An old college with later buildings and an almost melodramatic late 19th-century history (when there were public disputes over the election of a new Master), St Catharine's today presents an attractive face to Trumpington Street. Founded in 1473 for the study of theology and philosophy, its three-sided Principal Court was the work of Robert Grumbold, Sir Christopher Wren's mason. The college has since expanded on each side, incorporating the former Bull Hotel which had been left to St Catharine's in 1626. Beyond the Bull site the college developed the area along King's Lane jointly with King's College and, across the river, opened St Chad's Hostel in 1981. Here the accommodation consists of shared flatlets.

ST EDWARD'S CHURCH

St Edward's Passage
This church probably has Saxon origins, for it is dedicated to Edward the Confessor, the Saxon king. It has been much restored over the years, and the oldest remaining sections are the 13th-century tower and the chancel arch from around 1400. The two chapels on either side of the chancel were built for the members of Clare and Trinity Hall in the mid 15th century when their own church of St John Zachary was demolished to make way for King's College.

During the Reformation sermons were preached by Bilney, Barnes and Latimer from the early 16th-century pulpit which may still be seen in the church.

A memorial on the wall of St Botolph's Church. The date has worn away

The School of Pythagoras, one of Cambridge's oldest secular buildings

ST GILES' CHURCH

Castle Street/Chesterton Lane
Although the present church dates from the 19th century, it was rebuilt on the site of a Norman church. Built in an Early English style, the church incorporates the chancel arch from its predecessor. Despite the joining together of several parishes, the church became redundant, and is now used as a Brass Rubbing Centre.

ST JOHN'S COLLEGE

St John's Street
Neighbour to Trinity College and its rival in size and wealth, St John's is some 35 years older and more compact, though it extends over both sides of the river. Some of Cambridge's finest architecture, spanning many periods from the early 16th century to the 1960s, can be found in its nine courts.

St John's, like Christ's, was founded by Henry VII's mother, Lady Margaret Beaufort, and her coat of arms decorates the splendid early 16th-century gatehouse with its original oak doors. To this day the college boat club is called Lady Margaret, as is Cambridge's first professorship of divinity. Lady Margaret died in 1509, but Bishop John Fisher, her Confessor, carried out her intentions for the building of the college. First Court was built between 1511 and 1516, Second Court between 1598 and 1602, and their skyline reveals the changes in style. Outstanding is the gatehouse leading from Second to Third Court, the Shrewsbury Tower, so-called because Mary, Countess of Shrewsbury, partly paid for Second Court.

A real architectural contrast is revealed in Third Court: the Library on the north side was built in a

ST MARY THE GREAT CHURCH

See Great St Mary's Church

ST MARY THE LESS CHURCH

See Little St Mary's Church

ST MARY MAGDALENE CHAPEL

See Stourbridge Chapel

ST MICHAEL'S CHURCH

Trinity Street
This 14th-century Decorated Gothic building opposite Caius College retains its original quality in spite of restoration by Sir George Gilbert Scott in 1849 after a fire destroyed the roof. It was built in 1326 on the site of an earlier church, by Hervey de Stanton, founder of Michaelhouse, a college of 1324 now incorporated in Trinity College. It served both as parish church and as the college chapel. In 1966 the nave, which contains a full-length portrait of Charles I, became Great St Mary's parish hall. Worship continues in the larger chancel with 15th-century painted stalls, now St Michael's Chapel, and in Hervey de Stanton's south chapel with its ogee arched niches on either side of the east window.

ST PETER'S CHURCH

Castle Street
This tiny church, at less than 35ft long one of the smallest in the country, has a Norman font on which Tritons are carved— variously described as 'unusual decoration' or 'grotesque sculpture', depending on your taste. The church is of Norman foundation, with a 14th-century tower, but by the middle of the 18th century the building was no longer used for worship and stood roofless and windowless. It was rebuilt, on a reduced scale, in 1781, using materials from the old church. However, in the 20th century it once again is no longer in use and is in the hands of the Redundant Churches Fund.

SCOTT POLAR RESEARCH INSTITUTE (SPRI)

Lensfield Road
The Institute, an international centre for polar studies, was founded in memory of the explorer, Captain Robert Falcon Scott in 1920 and moved to its present building in 1934. The public museum, with its domed ceiling displaying maps of the Arctic and Antarctic, has fascinating examples of the cumbersome equipment carried on British polar explorations in the 19th and 20th centuries. Other smaller exhibits include arts and crafts of the polar regions, such as scrimshaw and Eskimo sculpture, and there are displays illustrating the wildlife of the region and modern scientific research.
    The Institute also has other collections not on public display, as well as a library containing the world's largest single collection of material on the polar regions, including hundreds of watercolours and thousands of photographs.

hybrid Tudor–Gothic style in the 1620s, the other two sides in a classical idiom between 1669 and 1673.
    Over the river, and behind the 19th-century New Court, are the two courts of the 1963–7 Cripps Building, quite the most outstanding of the three buildings with which the Cripps Foundation of Nottingham has endowed Cambridge. Powell and Moya, the architects, designed a zigzag which relates sympathetically to the river and to Bin-Brook, encloses a court behind New Court, and incorporates—a stroke of genius— two outstanding old buildings into a second court. The Norman 'School of Pythagoras', a house not a school, adjoins the gabled 17th-century Merton Hall.

The SPRI museum and (right) a close-up of the ceiling map of the Arctic

The massive iguanodon skeleton in the Sedgwick Museum of Geology

with a garden to the east, has a comfortable warmth. This is lacking in the 1966–8 Cripps Court off Cranmer Road.

SENATE HOUSE

King's Parade
James Gibbs' rectangular University 'parliament' building, lying alongside a grassy sward at the end of King's Parade, is certainly eye-catching. Built between 1722 and 1730, it successfully combines various classical styles—'a noble and complete entity' as one observer put it. The exterior suggests a building of considerable internal complexity, but the plan of the interior is actually quite simple—a hall with a small ante-chamber. The decoration, however, is elaborate, particularly the gallery around three sides and the panelling of the dais. Some of the interior woodwork is by James Essex senior. It is here that degrees are conferred and University policy is debated and put to the vote.

The Senate House is fronted by a well-manicured lawn, at the centre of which stands a copy in bronze of the huge Warwick Vase. It stands on a stone plinth pedestal which was inscribed by Eric Gill in 1936. The railings separating the lawn from King's Parade date from 1730, and are some of the earliest cast-iron railings in the country.

SHIRE HALL

Castle Street
This uncompromising rectangular building of 1932, facing Castle Mound, had a top storey added after World War II. All that remains of earlier buildings on the site is the

SEDGWICK MUSEUM OF GEOLOGY

Downing Street
Since 1904 this building, situated in the Downing Place corner of the Downing Street site, has housed the collection of fossils begun by Adam Sedgwick, Woodwardian Professor of Geology at Cambridge from 1818 to 1873. Clearly marked cases are arranged in order of geological time with appropriate fossils and casts. Special exhibits include a display on the evolution of the elephant family, and a reconstructed iguanodon skeleton. There are also skeletons of an Irish elk (bought for £140 in 1835) and of a hippopotamus from Barrington, near Cambridge, the latter providing a vivid reminder that the British climate has often changed over geological time.

At the far end of the displays is the Museum Woodwardian, claimed to be the oldest intact geological collection in the world, made by Dr John Woodward (1665–1728) and stored in its original walnut cabinets. Facing this is a fascinating display of Sedgwick's life and his contribution to geology.

SELWYN COLLEGE

Grange Road
Selwyn is a late 19th-century college, founded in memory of Bishop Selwyn of New Zealand and Lichfield with the aim of preserving Anglican values in the University. Until 1957 all Fellows, Scholars and Exhibitioners had to be Anglicans and Selwyn did not become a full member college of the University until this regulation was lifted. Sir Arthur Blomfield's Old Court with its outstanding chapel closed by an early 20th-century hall range and

recently cleaned old Police Station on Castle Street. In 1986–7 makeshift buildings at the back were cleared and an area as far as Victoria Road covered with a colourful complex of new buildings for the County Council's use and for business premises. This development is an interesting example of collaboration between local government and private enterprise.

SIDGWICK SITE

Between Sidgwick Avenue and West Road
In 1954 the University decided to develop this area as a centre for the

Shire Hall, the County Council's offices, as seen from Castle Mound

Stourbridge Chapel, part of the old leper hospital, may owe its survival to its use as a store for the Stourbridge Fair

arts faculties. Buildings include Lady Mitchell Hall, built in 1963–4 to seat 450, and named after the wife of Sir Godfrey Mitchell, chairman of the contractors, Wimpey. The name of the late 19th-century economist Alfred Marshall was given to the prestigious economics library.

One architectural firm, that run by Sir Hugh Cassons, planned the site but other architects were responsible for particular buildings within the overall plan. The most notorious is the triangular History Faculty building at the north-west corner, completed in 1968. James Stirling, the architect, has received international acclaim and rewards for this building, but the roof leaked, the glass cascade down the front made the library below oppressively hot and some of the harsh red bricks and tiles covering the sides fell off and have had to be replaced. At one time the University seriously considered pulling it down.

SIDNEY SUSSEX COLLEGE

Sidney Street
Sidney Sussex College is best known as Oliver Cromwell's college, and it possesses a contemporary portrait by Samuel Cooper and—more macabre—the Lord Protector's head, as a plaque in the ante-chapel records. The late 16th-century college, founded by Frances Sidney, Countess of Sussex, was transformed in 1831–2 by Sir Jeffrey Wyatville. He cement-rendered the Tudor–Gothic Hall Court and also Chapel Court where the chapel was rebuilt and the eastern range resurfaced. Although the façades of the two courts have now been modernised, the effect remains drab.

Two Civil War generals on opposite sides, George Goring the Royalist and the Parliamentarian Earl of Manchester, are amongst the past members of the college.

The bell-tower of Sidney Sussex College, a 16th-century foundation

The Norman door of Stourbridge Chapel

STOURBRIDGE CHAPEL

Newmarket Road
Stourbridge Chapel, the Leper Chapel, or, more correctly, St Mary Magdalene Chapel, is a fine example of Norman architecture. Built in the early 12th century, it was once the chapel for the leper hospital at Barnwell. The University took over the building early in the 19th century and kept it in good repair, as has the Cambridge Preservation Society in whose care it has been since 1954.

THEATRE ROYAL

See Festival Theatre

TRINITY COLLEGE

Trinity Street

Trinity is a royal college in several senses. It was founded by two kings, has housed royal undergraduates (Prince Charles was the most recent of these and his great-great-grandfather, later Edward VII, preceded him though he did not live in college), and the Master is not elected by the Fellows as in most colleges but appointed by the Crown. Recent incumbents have included G M Trevelyan, the historian and Macaulay's great-nephew, and R A Butler, the Conservative statesman.

Henry VIII created Trinity out of several pre-Reformation institutions, the main ones being King's Hall, Michaelhouse and Physwick Hostel. King's Hall had been founded about 200 years earlier by Edward III, but King's Hostel, a range extending north of Great Court, is all that remains of the 14th- to 15th-century college buildings. King Edward's Tower, built in 1428–32 as the gateway for King's Hall, and now the entrance to King's Hostel, became a model for later college gateways. Great Gate, the present entrance to Great Court, was also built for King's Hall, between 1490 and 1535. Since the early 17th century a statue of Henry VIII has stood in majesty over the gate, his majesty reduced, however, by the chair leg which replaces his sceptre. This was the result of a 20th-century student prank but is perhaps appropriate for the royal intruder in Edward III's place.

The fountain and hall in Trinity's Great Court, which both date from the early 17th century

Trinity straggles over a large area from Sidney Street to Grange Road but the heart of the college consists of Great Court and Nevile's Court, both the creation of Dr Thomas Nevile, Master from 1593 to 1615. Great Court, Cambridge's largest enclosed court, owes its charm to its very lack of symmetry, resulting from the welding together of buildings of different elevations and periods with a central focus in Nevile's 1601–2 fountain. Many later piecemeal alterations have given some uniformity to the court. The film *Chariots of Fire* has made famous Trinity's undergraduate challenge—completing a run round the court while the clock strikes midnight. Trinity's chapel, on the north side of Great Court, cannot compete with that of King's, but it is an interesting Counter-Reformation building in Gothic style begun in Mary I's reign, with an 18th-century screen and stalls. In the ante-chapel is Roubiliac's statue of Isaac Newton and statues of Francis Bacon, Macaulay and Tennyson. Great Court also contains the Judges' Suite in its north-west corner. This is where, in the past, judges arriving for the Assizes would be accommodated.

Beyond Great Court is Nevile's Court with one of Cambridge's major buildings on its western side. This is Sir Christopher Wren's Library of 1676–95, a striking contrast with the Elizabethan Hall opposite. The Library has two aspects, to Nevile's Court and to the river; the façades have a subtle external design which conceals the internal floor level. The Library not only contains a fine collection of books and manuscripts but also busts and statues of some of the college's famous students.

Principal Court of Trinity Hall. It was originally a law college

TRINITY HALL

Trinity Lane

Its compact situation between Trinity Lane and the river, and Clare College and Garret Hostel Lane gives Trinity Hall a friendly atmosphere. Founded in 1350 by William Bateman, Bishop of Norwich, it was originally known as 'The College of the Scholars of the Holy Trinity of Norwich'. Principal Court was built in the college's early days, but 18th-century ashlar now disguises it. The college chapel has a fine plaster ceiling and brasses. Fourteenth-century clunch and red brick can be seen in the north wall of Principal Court. From the west of North Court a staircase leads to an imaginative 20th-century range by Wyn Roberts and Geoffrey Clarke where a flower-decked terrace outside a bar and lecture room faces the gardens. Below is the Elizabethan library with its original desks, shelves and chained books.

The 150ft-long Wren Library at Trinity College seen from the river

UNION SOCIETY, THE

Bridge Street
Behind the Round Church is a multi-coloured brick building which has served as a political nursery for many of Britain's outstanding politicians. Built by Alfred Waterhouse in 1866, the club facilities, library and debating chamber—which is a miniature of the House of Commons save for its gallery—have provided a discussion forum for over 120 years. In 1866 the Society was already some 50 years old although it had been suppressed in 1817 because it discussed politics! However this has been the life-blood of debates ever since, together with forays into awkward cultural and social issues.

UNIVERSITY LIBRARY, THE

West Road
There has been a University Library in Cambridge for nearly 600 years. Since 1662 it has been entitled to receive free a copy of every book published in the United Kingdom and is now one of five copyright libraries in the country. For many centuries the library was housed in the Old Schools but, despite frequent additions to the space available, it still outgrew its accommodation. The present building with its 160ft-high tower, designed by Sir Giles Gilbert Scott, was opened in 1934 by George V, and in 1972 a large extension was added. The Reading Room, which is about 190ft long, houses only a minute fraction of the millions of books contained in the library.

WESTMINSTER COLLEGE

Madingley Road
The red-brick college which closes the view at the northern end of Queen's Road is the grandest of five independent theological colleges. Opened in 1899 for a London Presbyterian college founded in 1844, in 1967 it absorbed Cheshunt, the oldest Cambridge theological college, which was situated in Bateman Street near the Botanic Garden.

WHIPPLE MUSEUM OF THE HISTORY OF SCIENCE

Free School Lane
R S Whipple's collection began the museum in 1944 and in 1952 it moved into the old Perse School hall which was restored in 1976. Among

The Union Society, one of a number of Cambridge buildings designed by Alfred Waterhouse, has been enlarged several times since

much else the hall contains early surveying equipment (theodolite and chain), navigation instruments (astrolobes, quadrants and sextants), and a grand orrery—a clockwork model of the planetary system—dating from about 1750 flanked by two globes. In a second room microscopes, chemical balances and fascinating electrostatic generators can be seen.

Some of the scientific instruments displayed in the Whipple Museum

WOLFSON COLLEGE

Barton Road
In 1965 University College, a graduate foundation, was set up by the University in Bredon House, Selwyn Gardens. However, a grant from the Wolfson Foundation in 1972 transformed the site, and the name was changed accordingly. The traditional layout, in courts, has been achieved by uniting the existing house with new ranges, some of stone, others of mixed shades of brick. Thin slabs of granite, from parts of the stonework of London Bridge, were used to floor the entrance hall.

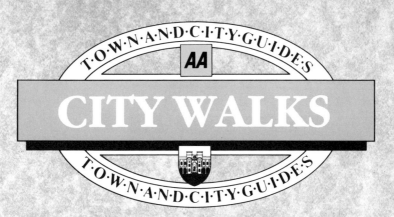

CITY WALKS

*The timber-framed gallery of the President's Lodge, Queens'
College, where The Master was able to take a daily stroll
whatever the weather*

Below the Castle

This walk, in the northern part of the city, takes in many of the sites important in Cambridge's early history, as well as a 20th-century art gallery. It also includes a visit to Castle Mound, with its views over the whole city.

The Norman Round Church, which was heavily restored in the 19th century

---

Allow 1 hour

Start at the Round Church and continue north-westwards along Bridge Street.

1 ROUND CHURCH
Built in 1130, this is the oldest of only four surviving round churches in England. The style was introduced by the returning crusaders in remembrance of the Church of the Holy Sepulchre in Jerusalem.

2 BRIDGE STREET
Finely renovated buildings on the right of this street make it possible to re-create mentally the scene of medieval Cambridge. This was the main street, following the line of the earlier Roman road, leading to the Great Bridge. It housed many more traders than today, and several inns and stables. The alley between the two pubs, the Mitre and the Baron of Beef, once led to a courtyard containing 11 houses and, 400 years ago, a brewery. Before the church, on your right, look above the door of the clothes shop to see the three balls of the pawnbroker's symbol; not the commonplace sign it was many years ago.
Immediately before the church turn right into Portugal Place.

3 PORTUGAL PLACE
St Clement's Church, dating from the early 13th century, marks the entry to this peaceful residential quarter so close to the city centre. Much has changed here since medieval times, when thatched cottages housed boatmen and college servants. Many properties, however, are still owned by the colleges; nowadays they are used to accommodate students. The exclusion of vehicles (bar the odd bicycle) has long been enforced, as the police notice at the end of the street on the wall of 10 Portugal Street bears out.
Continue into Portugal Street, turn left along Park Parade, then right to follow the riverside path on Jesus Green to the lock. Here cross the footbridge and turn left. At the traffic-lights at the end of Chesterton Lane turn right into Castle Street, past St Giles' Church on the corner.

4 ST GILES' CHURCH
A church has stood here since Norman times, but nothing now remains of the original building although the chancel arch dates back to the Norman period. This is the oldest part of Cambridge, where the Romans first mounted guard over their river crossing at the foot of the hill. Long after the Romans departed, the higher ground on this side of the river made it a natural point for defence and settlement.
Opposite the church stands the Cambridge and County Folk Museum.

5 FOLK MUSEUM
Until 1934 this was the White Horse Inn, one of 11 pubs in the street during the last century. A wide chimney-breast, now blocked up, provided a hiding hole—popular no doubt with the highwaymen of earlier days. In keeping with its original use, the museum contains a Bar Parlour Room, along with other domestic reminders of the past.
Continue up the hill, past St Peter's Church on the left.

A badge exhibited in the Cambridge and County Folk Museum

6 ST PETER'S CHURCH
A population decline in the parish has left this little church in the hands of the Redundant Churches Fund. Although built in the early 12th century, Roman bricks (looking like rough red tiles) can be seen built into the walls by the main door. Until 1802 a gaol existed close by, and many an escaping prisoner is said to have clung to the altar rails seeking sanctuary in this church.
Castle Mound lies further up Castle Street, in the grounds of Shire Hall.

7 CASTLE MOUND
Climb to the top for a view of the Cambridge skyline, contrasting the medieval spires of colleges with later

Looking north along Bridge Street

The buildings at Kettle's Yard, now used to house a modern art gallery

buildings such as the University Library. The mound is all that is left of the Norman castle, built first in wood and then in stone. It was little used after the 15th century, and its walls were dismantled with the stone being used instead for some of the college buildings.

Turn left off Castle Street into Whymans Lane. A pub, The Three Tuns, once stood in front of Bell's Court and was a favourite haunt of highwayman Dick Turpin. Continue down Pound Hill and at the bottom bear left into Northampton Street to Kettle's Yard Gallery.

8 KETTLE'S YARD

The area known as Kettle's Yard used to be occupied by a number of

9 MAGDALENE COLLEGE

This was the last college to surrender its all-male status but will admit women after 1988. It is particularly famous for the library collection of Samuel Pepys, a former member of the college. The picturesque timber-framed buildings on the west side of the road are all owned by Magdalene too. Had the college not run out of money in 1930 they would have been demolished to make way for a grand new court, but fortunately they have survived, preserving another medieval reminder of old Cambridge.

Continue over the bridge.

10 THE BRIDGE

The river was first forded at this point by the Romans, so that their great road, *Via Devana*, could continue from Colchester to Chester. Saxons, Danes and Normans have all settled at this focal point, as Cambridge grew into an important inland port. Various bridges have, at times, spanned the river, the first believed to have been built before 875. Nowadays punts are the only river traffic to float gently under the bridge.

Continue along Magdalene Street and Bridge Street back to the Round Church.

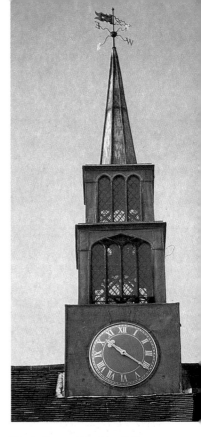

The clocktower at Magdalene College

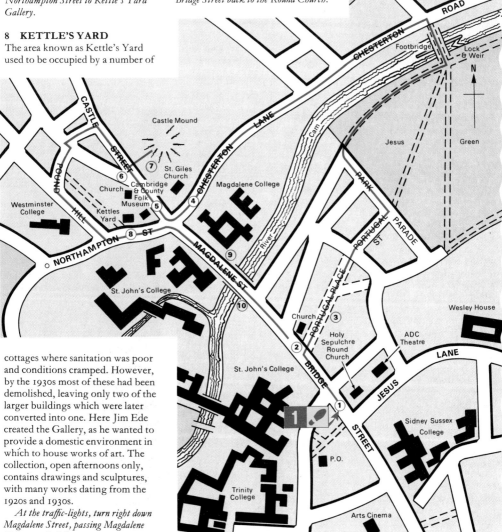

cottages where sanitation was poor and conditions cramped. However, by the 1930s most of these had been demolished, leaving only two of the larger buildings which were later converted into one. Here Jim Ede created the Gallery, as he wanted to provide a domestic environment in which to house works of art. The collection, open afternoons only, contains drawings and sculptures, with many works dating from the 1920s and 1930s.

At the traffic-lights, turn right down Magdalene Street, passing Magdalene College on the left.

Market Square to Midsummer Common

*F*rom *the very centre of the city, this walk follows the southern limit of the medieval town, passes three colleges, crosses Jesus Green and returns along one of the main shopping streets.*

Allow 1½ hours

Start in the Market Square.

1 MARKET SQUARE
The original market-place, an L-shaped area at the very heart of the medieval town, was smaller than the present one, trading mainly in corn, poultry, meat and butter. It has been

Plaque on Fisher House, the RC chaplaincy of the University

the scene of many an event over the centuries, not least the Great Fire of 1849 which destroyed many of the surrounding buildings and resulted in today's open market-place. The fire raged through the night, and lines of men supplied buckets of water from as far away as the river. Now the market sells an enormous range of goods, but continues to be a colourful and thriving affair.

Facing the Guildhall, walk round the building to the right, and turn into Peas Hill.

2 PEAS HILL
This area may appear flat, but in early days it was much higher than the surrounding marshy ground. Peas Hill was, in the past, well-known for its many fish stalls. Beneath this area is a vast network of cellars and tunnels covering a quarter of an acre, which have at times been used as wine vaults, and then as air-raid shelters during World War II.

Turn right into Bene't Street, then left before St Bene't's Church into Free School Lane.

3 ST BENE'T'S CHURCH
The tower of the church dates back to Saxon times and is the oldest surviving building in the county. The church served as a chapel for

Corpus Christi College, next door, and a gallery connecting the two can still be seen from the lane.

Continue along Free School Lane, passing the Whipple Museum of the History of Science on the left.

4 FREE SCHOOL LANE
During its long history the Free School Lane area has housed an Augustinian friary, the old Botanic Garden, lecture rooms and the famous Cavendish Laboratory, as well as the Perse School which probably gave the road its name. The Whipple Museum, situated in the old school hall, has many fine exhibits relating to the scientific background of this site.

At the end of the road turn left into Downing Street. This follows the line of the King's Ditch, marking the southern boundary of medieval Cambridge. On reaching St Andrew's Street turn left; on the other side of the street is Emmanuel College.

5 EMMANUEL COLLEGE
Like several of the other colleges, Emmanuel was built on the site of a friary which was established here from the 13th century until its dissolution in 1538. Some of the old monastic buildings were adapted to college life. The present chapel was added a little later and was designed by Christopher Wren.

Continue northwards along St Andrew's Street to Christ's College and St Andrew the Great Church.

6 CHRIST'S COLLEGE AND ST ANDREW THE GREAT CHURCH
The King's Ditch, famous more for its unsanitary nature than defensive potential, followed a line from Downing Street along to Hobson Street. At this point the ditch crossed close to Barnwell Gate, one of the main entrances to the town. The church at this junction, known previously as St Andrew without Barnwell Gate, contains a memorial to Captain Cook, whose widow and two sons are buried here. Christ's College opposite, founded by Lady Beaufort, has many famous past students including John Milton and Charles Darwin.

Bear right along Hobson Street which turns right into King Street.

7 KING STREET
This street has changed considerably over the years, especially on its

Lady Beaufort's coat of arms on the gatehouse of Christ's College

northern side where the colleges have built new residences for students. Previously, it had the atmosphere of village life, with small shops, almshouses and many pubs, the last-mentioned resulting in the 'King Street Run', a University tradition to attempt to drink a glass of beer in each of the 13 or 14 pubs before closing time. Only five pubs now remain, the Champion of the Thames being the oldest.

At the roundabout, cross to Victoria Avenue, with Jesus College on the left and Midsummer Common on the right.

8 MIDSUMMER COMMON
Before enclosure, this was an area of open pasture, dissected by ditches and meandering tracks. A fair has been held on the common every midsummer since the 13th century and although the fair today has

A view along Free School Lane

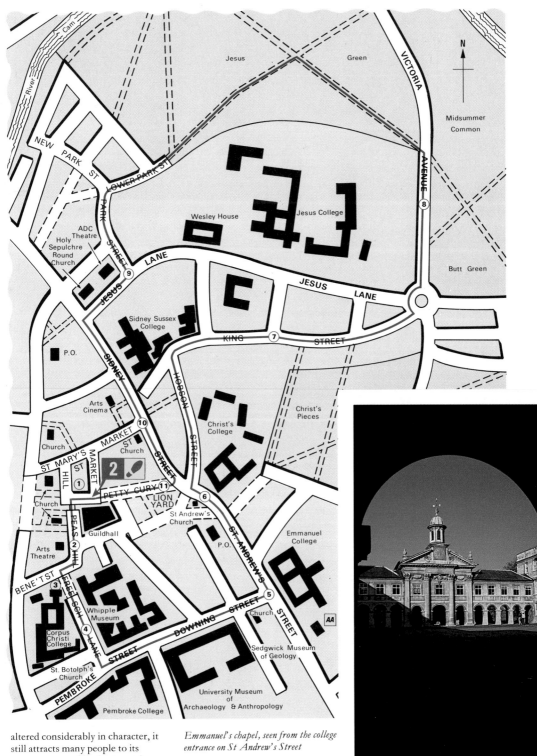

Emmanuel's chapel, seen from the college entrance on St Andrew's Street

altered considerably in character, it still attracts many people to its amusements and lively atmosphere.

Turn left along the path at the end of Jesus College onto Jesus Green. At the cross-roads in the middle of the Green take the left-hand path. Continue down Lower Park Street, left into Park Street, and at the junction with Jesus Lane turn right past the Pitt Club.

9 PITT CLUB
The classical frontage of this building may seem surprising when compared to its neighbours, until you consider it was built in the mid 19th century to house a mock Roman Bath. However, the scheme did not last long as the premises were taken over by the political Pitt

Club in 1866. The building's function has again diversified; part of it is now used as a restaurant.

Turn left into Sidney Street.

10 SIDNEY STREET
Sidney Street was one of the principal routes through the town, following the line of the Roman road towards the bridge over the Cam. Now it is a busy shopping street, retaining some of the outfitters and older stores that gave it an atmosphere of some elegance during the 19th century.

Just before returning to the junction

with Hobson Street turn right into Petty Cury.

11 PETTY CURY/LION YARD
The Lion Yard shopping complex on the left retains nothing of the architecture, alleyways or cobble-stones that characterised the area until the mid 20th century. There used to be numerous coaching inns here too, and it was the largest of these, the Red Lion, which gave its name to the modern development.

Continue along Petty Cury to return to the Market Square.

The Fitzwilliam and the Cam

A short walk, taking in four colleges, the splendid Fitzwilliam Museum, the upper river and some of the city's quieter—but just as fascinating—back streets.

Allow 1 hour

Start at the corner of Mill Lane and Trumpington Street where the University Press Building stands.

1 UNIVERSITY PRESS (PITT) BUILDING

Printing was an early industry in Cambridge, starting in 1521. The first publications were mostly Bibles and prayer books, although works such as Newton's *Principia* appeared by the 18th century. This imposing church-like building dating from 1833 housed the University Press until recently, and still has a showroom and offices.

One of several Catherine wheels to be seen at St Catharine's College

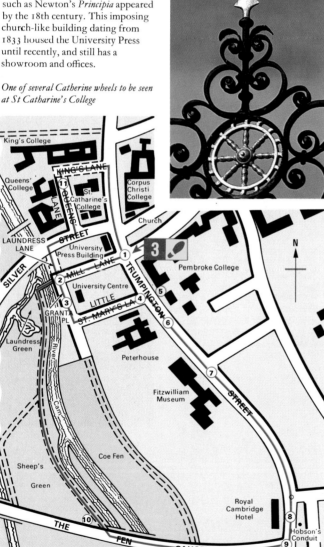

Walk down Mill Lane—passing University lecture halls and other departments—to the Mill Pond.

2 MILL POND

This tranquil spot was once a busy wharf area with barges bringing goods and grains to the mills which stood here. This was as far inland as boats could travel, thus establishing Cambridge as an important trading centre. Until the arrival of the railway in 1845 the river was a vital link for transporting goods.

Turn left at the bottom of Mill Lane passing the University Centre on the left.

3 UNIVERSITY CENTRE

The modern building overlooking the Mill Pond is used by graduates for recreational and social functions. Here a row of cottages once stood, whose tenants provided a laundry service for the University. Husbands and sons would collect washing from the colleges, wives and daughters would wash and iron. The open space over the river is known as Laundress Green, where lines of washing drying in the wind used to be a familiar sight.

Shortly turn left into Little St Mary's Lane, past a row of charming old houses to Little St Mary's Church.

4 LITTLE ST MARY'S CHURCH

Built between 1340 and 1352, this church replaced an older one dedicated to St Peter. Peterhouse, next door, was the first college to be founded in Cambridge, and took its name from the church. Inside is a gallery connecting the two buildings, designed to prevent students 'losing' themselves between study and prayer. To the left of the entrance is a plaque in memory of the Reverend Godfrey Washington who belonged to the same family as the American, George Washington. The churchyard is one of the most peaceful in Cambridge.

Cross Trumpington Street to Pembroke College.

5 WREN CHAPEL
The chapel of Pembroke College is the first completed work of Sir Christopher Wren, built in 1663–4 in pure classical style. His uncle, the Bishop of Ely, was imprisoned in the Tower of London during the Civil War, and vowed—should he be released—to thank the Almighty in some way. To this end, he asked his nephew to design the college chapel.

On leaving Pembroke turn left down Trumpington Street towards Peterhouse.

6 PETERHOUSE
Peterhouse dates from the late 13th century. In the 18th century the poet Thomas Gray was a student at the college and the window from which he is reputed to have escaped down a rope-ladder into a tub of water put there by fellow students (see page 29) can be seen top left.

Further along Trumpington Street is the imposing building of the Fitzwilliam Museum.

7 FITZWILLIAM MUSEUM
This temple to the Arts was opened to the public in 1848. Richard, 7th Viscount Fitzwilliam, bequeathed to the University his library of 10,000 books, paintings and manuscripts. Income from investments was to provide a building to house the collection and to buy new works. The contents of the museum are now vast, and many items are housed in the modern extension which was constructed in keeping with the original design of the building.

The gutters running along both sides of

Left: the University Press Building, designed by Edward Blore

the street were used to bring fresh water to the town. *Continue to Hobson's Conduit at the corner of Lensfield Road.*

8 HOBSON'S CONDUIT
The conduit used to stand in the Market Square where it marked the end of the artificial watercourse, built jointly by the town and University to bring fresh water from springs outside the town. In its original position the conduit was surrounded by railings to which, it has been recorded, offenders who had been sentenced to a public whipping were chained.

Just past the Royal Cambridge Hotel turn right down Fen Causeway. The Leys School stands to the left.

9 LEYS SCHOOL
Founded in the mid-1870s, this was the first public school to be set up by the Methodist Church—in order to rival those of the Church of England. The famous book *Goodbye Mr Chips* was written by a master of the Leys, who based his character on a colleague at the school. It remained an all-boys' institution until 1984, when girls were admitted to the sixth form.

Continue along the Causeway, turn

Above: the Mathematical Bridge at Queens' College which can be seen from Silver Street if you make a slight detour to the left

Left: Margaret of Anjou's coat of arms in Queens' College First Court

right just after the river bridge and walk along the footpath looking across to Coe Fen.

10 COE FEN
This area of common fen land, so close to the city centre, gives an idea of how difficult it would have been to extend building during medieval times. The low-lying meadow land is still prone to flooding, but provides the unusual city-centre sight of grazing cattle and wild flowers.

Follow the path back to the Mill Pond, cross the weir and turn left down Laundress Lane. Note the public notice on the wall dated 1857. Turn right into Silver Street, then left along Queens' Lane.

11 QUEENS' LANE
This quiet, narrow lane was once the southern end of 'Milne Street', the main street of early Cambridge which led down to the wharfs and King's Mill. Queens' College on the left has buildings dating back to 1448 including one of the few half-timbered structures in the colleges. St Catharine's College on the right was built facing onto this busy street, but changed its entrance to Trumpington Street when the lane declined in importance.

Turn right at the end of the lane, go through the passage-way to Trumpington Street, then turn right again back to the start of the walk.

Buildings Old and New

As the University grew, the town centre became a crowded jumble of buildings. From the hustle and bustle of this busy area, the walk passes by the more recent buildings west of the river, returning via the Backs.

Allow ¼ hour

Start at the junction of King's Parade and Bene't Street and walk south along Trumpington Street.

1 TRUMPINGTON STREET
Unlike other medieval colleges, Corpus Christi—on the left—was founded by townspeople rather than a monarch or famous person. As well as famed scholars, the college also has a ghost! One story tells of the Master's daughter hiding her student lover in a spring-loaded chest. He died of suffocation, she of a broken heart, and his spirit is said to haunt the Old Court. Opposite is St Catharine's College where in order to build the three-sided courtyard a row of 17th-century inns was demolished. One of these was owned by Thomas Hobson, who also hired out horses. He always insisted on the horse nearest the door being taken, hence the expression 'Hobson's Choice'—or lack of!

Continue to St Botolph's Church at the end of Silver Street.

2 ST BOTOLPH'S CHURCH
In medieval times this church lay close to the southern gates of the town, hence its dedication to St Botolph, the patron saint of travellers. In the attractive churchyard is a memorial to James Essex Junior, a notable 18th-century architect who designed buildings for many of the older colleges.

Turn right down Silver Street.

3 SILVER STREET BRIDGE
Passing Queens' Lane, formerly a main street, on the right, we come to the river and a crossing point of some importance at a time when Cambridge thrived on its river trade. Long before the colleges were built, barges brought grain to the wharfs and mills that stood around the Mill Pond. The wooden bridge that now connects the old and new

The present St Botolph's Church dates back to the 14th century. Inset: sundials on the tower

buildings of Queens' College (on the right) is the Mathematical Bridge. Legend says it was constructed on geometrical principles, but when taken apart for further investigation, it proved too complicated to rebuild without the help of the odd bolt or nail.

Further along, on the left, is Darwin College.

4 DARWIN COLLEGE

Darwin, one of five Cambridge colleges for post-graduate students only, was founded in 1964. In the days before it became a college one of Charles Darwin's sons lived here, in the centre house. The book *Period Piece* by Gwen Raverat, grand-daughter of Darwin, was written here and describes life in this house during the 1880s.

After passing Darwin, continue across the traffic-lights and up Sidgwick Avenue to the Sidgwick Site on the right.

5 SIDGWICK SITE

During the second half of the 19th century, student numbers increased rapidly and in the congested town centre it was impossible to find extra teaching space or accommodation. New colleges were therefore built to the west of the river (Newnham in 1875, Selwyn in 1882) as was extra housing for Dons who, after 1882,

were permitted to marry. Further development of the area continued in the 20th century.

Turn right through the Sidgwick Site, under the walkway of the modern teaching blocks, to the Faculty of History.

6 FACULTY OF HISTORY

Completed in 1968, this modern glass-faced building by James Stirling has caused more controversy than most. For some it is bold and exciting, for others brutal and without constraint. It has also suffered many problems such as leaking roofs and peeling tiles and brickwork. Despite all this, it remains one of the most eye-catching buildings of the modern University.

Continue along the footpath, crossing West Road onto the playing fields of King's College School, to the University Library.

7 UNIVERSITY LIBRARY

In addition to college and faculty libraries, nearly every student spends some time amongst the four million books housed here. It is one of the few copyright libraries in the country entitled to receive, free, a copy of every book published in

The river and punt landing-stage at King's College

Britain. As a result, the 45 miles of shelving originally built in 1934 have already been considerably extended.

Turn right down Burrell's Walk, cross Queen's Road and follow the footpath to the right, along by the stream through the Backs.

8 THE BACKS

It is unusual to find stretches of open meadow, pleasant walks and gardens so close to a city centre. This land is, however, owned by the colleges which 'back' onto the river. Two clearly distinguishable areas of raised ground opposite King's College are all that remains of a causeway that once crossed the river to a parish church standing where King's Lawn is today.

Turn left through the back gate of King's College, cross over the river and go through to the front entrance of the college to return to King's Parade.

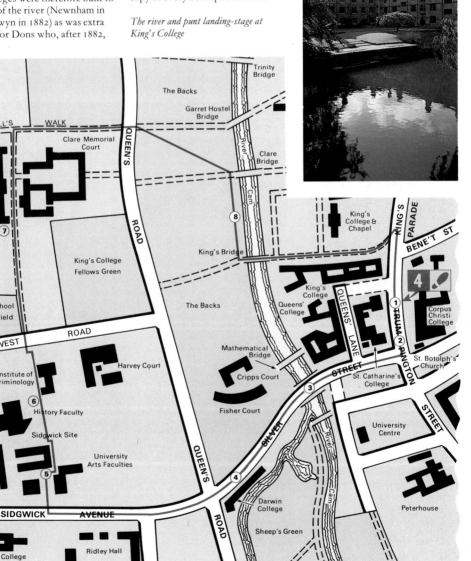

Five Colleges and a Chapel

*T**his walk passes through some of the most famous of the riverside colleges and visits beautiful King's College Chapel. During May access is restricted because of student examinations and it may be difficult to follow the route exactly.*

Allow 1¼ hours

Start at the King's Parade/Bene't Street junction and walk along King's Parade towards the Senate House.

The Bridge of Sighs, linking the two parts of St John's College

1 KING'S PARADE

This much-photographed street contains many oddments of interest as well as a wealth of history. King's College, with its Chapel, is the obvious focal-point—but outside, notice the post-box dating back to Victorian times. The buildings opposite have a mixture of styles and functions and are owned by various colleges. Above the shops is student accommodation, added to piecemeal over the years, hence the variety in height of the buildings. At the end of the row is Ryder and Amis, an outfitters specialising in academic dress for all occasions. Displayed in the window are fixture lists for college matches. Great St Mary's Church, next door, is the University Church. The stone circle on the right-hand buttress is the point from which all distances locally are measured, and at one time there was a regulation that all students had to live within three miles of this circle.

2 SENATE HOUSE

Built in the 1720s, this is one of the few purely classical buildings in Cambridge. It serves as a meeting place, debating chamber and stage for one of the University's most colourful ceremonies—Degree Day. It has also been the target of student pranks. One night a car appeared on the roof of the Senate House—it took a week for the authorities to work out how to get it down.

Turn left down Senate House Passage.

3 SENATE HOUSE PASSAGE

It is said the cobbles on the left are the property of the University, on the right of Gonville and Caius College, and the central slabs are the property of the town! Sundials crown the Gate of Honour (to the right), the final of the three 'gates' which a Caius student would pass through on his 'path' to a degree.

At the end of the passage turn left into Trinity Lane.

4 TRINITY LANE

At a time when Cambridge prospered on its river trade, this tiny lane was part of the main street of the town. However, when Henry VI decided to build his huge chapel at King's, he cleared a large part of central Cambridge, demolishing houses and interrupting the line of this street.

Turn right through Clare College.

The fountain in Trinity's Great Court

5 CLARE COLLEGE

This college was re-founded by Elizabeth de Clare in 1338, when the original (1326) buildings were destroyed by fire. Some say the present style is more like a palace than a college. The bridge over the river is the oldest one remaining today. To the right, beyond the bridge, is the Fellows' Garden.

Go right through the back gate of the college and right again to cross Garret Hostel Bridge.

6 TRINITY HALL

The gateway in Garret Hostel Lane once stood at the front of the college and was used as an alternative entrance at a time when much friction existed between 'town' and 'gown'. In peaceful periods the main gate was open, allowing horse and cart to enter, but if trouble arose, the smaller gate gave quick access to a man on horseback. During riots only the inner gate was opened leaving just enough room for a man to run in to the safety of the college.

Turn left into Trinity Lane, then right. At the junction, follow Trinity Street left to the main gate of Trinity College.

7 TRINITY COLLEGE

Founded by Henry VIII, Trinity College stands on the site of earlier colleges and hostels. One of these, King's Hall, was initiated by Edward III and his coat of arms can be seen above the gate along with those of his six sons. One of these shields is blank, as this son died before the arms could be presented. The statue is of Henry VIII, the target of yet another student prank. In his hand is not a sceptre, but a chair leg! On the right of the gate is a small apple tree which is said to have been grown from the seedling of the tree that inspired Newton's theory of gravity.

Enter the Great Court.

8 GREAT COURT

This is the largest private enclosed court in the country and it is a college tradition to try to run around its perimeter before the clock strikes 12 (it takes 43 seconds). Lord Byron was a student at Trinity

and is said to have taken baths in the fountain and kept a bear as a pet. Prince Charles also studied here.

Climb the steps on the far side of the court and go past the dining hall into Nevile's Court where the Wren Library can be seen.

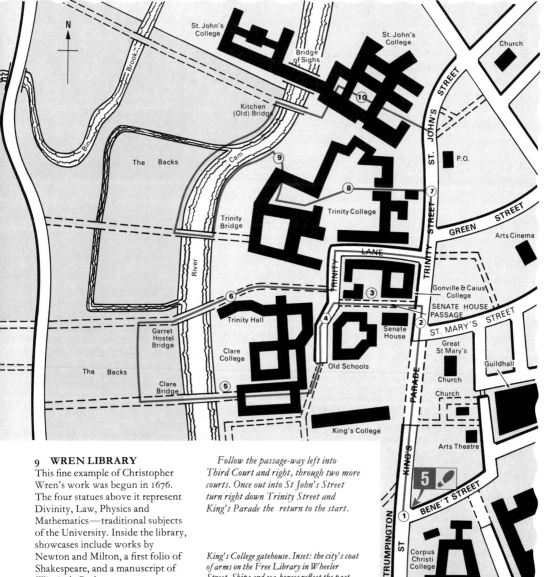

9 WREN LIBRARY

This fine example of Christopher Wren's work was begun in 1676. The four statues above it represent Divinity, Law, Physics and Mathematics—traditional subjects of the University. Inside the library, showcases include works by Newton and Milton, a first folio of Shakespeare, and a manuscript of *Winnie the Pooh*.

Leave by the back gate, walk left alongside the river and cross Trinity Bridge. Turn right and continue on the path, over a stream, then re-cross the river, via Kitchen Bridge, into St John's College grounds.

10 ST JOHN'S COLLEGE

To the left of the river is New Court, built in neo-Gothic style in the late 1820s. Its shape, with the high central section, is often referred to as 'the wedding cake'. As you re-cross the river at Kitchen Bridge you can see the so-called Bridge of Sighs built in 1831 to connect New Court with the older buildings. One year students floated a car upriver on four punts and, under cover of darkness, left it suspended beneath the bridge.

Follow the passage-way left into Third Court and right, through two more courts. Once out into St John's Street turn right down Trinity Street and King's Parade the return to the start.

King's College gatehouse. Inset: the city's coat of arms on the Free Library in Wheeler Street. Ships and sea-horses reflect the past

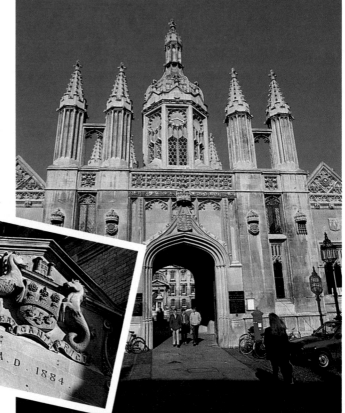

The Path to Grantchester

T̄his pleasant walk passes through the suburbs of Newnham and crosses the Cam's delightful river meadows, ending up at the well-known village of Grantchester beloved by Rupert Brooke.

Allow 1 hour (one-way)

Start at the cross-roads where Queen's Road meets Silver Street. Walk south down Newnham Road, past the pond and over the roundabout, keeping the green, Lammas Land, on your left.

LAMMAS LAND

The word 'Lammas' comes from the Old English, *llaf*, meaning loaf or bread, and *maesse*, meaning mass. Lammas Day, 1 August, was a harvest festival. From this date until early spring all Lammas Lands became open for the 'commoners' to graze their livestock upon. No one exercises this customary right now, but the area remains an open space to be used by the public at all times of year.

NEWNHAM

This suburb of Cambridge was just a hamlet in pre-Conquest days, but was probably settled as early as Saxon times. It stood on slightly higher ground and was the site of a land grant for a Carmelite friary in about 1250. Prior to that, the *Domesday Book* records the existence of a mill, which reflects the importance of Cambridge as an inland port. Field paths would have connected Newnham to Cambridge. By the end of the 15th century the Carmelites had moved closer to the town, and Newnham remained a small settlement until the expansion of the University in the late 19th century. It is now considered to be one of the more desirable areas of Cambridge in which to live.

Continue down Grantchester Street. At the end follow the signpost to the footpath which runs alongside the river to Grantchester.

Right: attractive thatched cottages in Grantchester, which is situated about two miles south of Cambridge

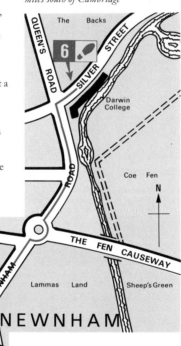

Go through the gate at the end of the footpath, along the lane, then turn left and follow the road around the bend, past The Old Vicarage.

THE OLD VICARAGE

This is the setting of the famous poem by Rupert Brooke, written in 1912. A student and later Fellow at King's College, he left his lodgings there to live at The Orchard, and later moved to The Old Vicarage as a paying guest in 1910. In recent years the vicarage has had another well-known occupant, the author and politician Jeffrey Archer.

Follow the footpath along the side of the house to the mill pond.

GRANTCHESTER MILL

The river here was once busy with barges travelling upriver to the mill. However, the original building was destroyed by fire in 1928 and has been rebuilt as a house. Only punts now venture this far, and it is a peaceful spot for anglers, visitors and aspiring poets!

Turn right, following the road back to the village and the church.

GRANTCHESTER MEADOWS

The riverside meadows are a popular place, especially in summer, for an easy stroll to Grantchester village. Although commonly known as the Cam, an earlier name for the river was the Granta. The name is Celtic in origin, probably meaning 'fen river' or 'muddy river', which it certainly is. In season, punts pass up and down the river, though for the inexperienced this method of transport can often prove harder work, and more hazardous, than walking. As you look back towards Cambridge, the pinnacles of King's College Chapel and other landmarks are visible above the treeline.

The Rupert Brooke pub in Grantchester, named after the village's most famous resident

Byron is said to have swum in this pool, named after him, in Grantchester

PARISH CHURCH

A church has stood on this site since the 11th century, when Grantchester was a tiny village built on the higher ground above the river. As in other settlements, it was the focal point of village life. The present building dates from the late 14th century and is particularly noted for its fine chancel. In the churchyard a war memorial bears the name of Rupert Brooke, amongst others. The church's clock is, perhaps, its best-known feature, quoted many a time in the closing lines of Brooke's poem

. . . **Oh yet
Stands the Church clock at ten
to three?
And is there honey still for tea?**

Continue through the village, returning to Cambridge either by road or back along the footpath. Alternatively, by planning ahead, a bus can be taken back to the city centre.

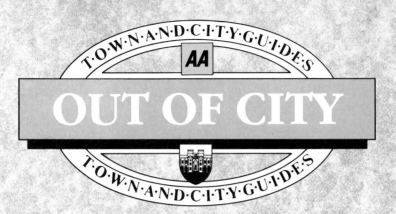

OUT OF CITY

*Extraordinary religious carvings – perhaps the work of the
Knights Templar – adorn the chalk walls of Royston Cave
in Hertfordshire*

ANGLESEY ABBEY

98TL5362

This house, on the outskirts of the hamlet of Lode, retains a few arches from the original 13th-century Augustinian priory but most of the fabric had gone when a house was built on the site in about 1600. Amongst the owners have been Thomas Hobson, the Cambridge carrier, and Sir George Downing, founder of the Cambridge college that bears his name. The present building took its shape and style in the 20th century from the work of Lord Fairhaven, who made it the home of his collection of pictures and *objets d'art*, still displayed in the house. He also created the wonderful Georgian-style gardens which combine formal and landscape elements, and are set with urns and statues.

ASHWELL

98TL2639

In the centre of this attractive village, situated very close to the junction of the counties of Cambridgeshire, Bedfordshire and Hertfordshire, the springs which supply the River Cam bubble out in a little dell. The village itself was an important town when *Domesday Book* was written, with a weekly market and four annual fairs. Since then it has been supplanted by other towns, but a number of medieval houses survive, one of which contains the village museum. The church, mostly dating from the 14th century, has an unusual collection of medieval graffiti. The most notable records the horror of the plague in 1350, a grim thought in this now tranquil place.

Gateway to the ironworks at Bedford. The works were opened in 1859 by the Howard family

AUDLEY END HOUSE

98TL5237

The imposing front of this 17th-century house looks across a landscaped park to the road. The estate, once that of a priory, was granted to Sir Thomas Audley (the same that refounded Magdalene College in Cambridge) at the time of the Dissolution of the Monasteries. His house was rebuilt by his grandson around 1610, and was nearly three times the size it is today. The main hall has rich Jacobean decoration, but owes some of its features to later (*c.*1720) work by Sir John Vanbrugh. Vanbrugh also advised the demolition of the second court. Later in the century Robert Adam carried out renovations to a set of rooms and also designed features for the grounds—the Temple of Concord, the Tea House Bridge and the Adam Bridge. Capability Brown landscaped the park itself. The stables at Audley End now house a collection of farm implements, and there is also a miniature railway in the grounds.

BEDFORD

96TL0449

The modern shopping centre reveals little of the past of this town which traces its origins back to Saxon times, but by the riverside are several features of historical interest. A mound is the only trace left of the Norman castle, and gardens now occupy the site which also houses the Cecil Higgins Museum, a collection of art treasures. On the Embankment is

The palatial Audley End House with its Jacobean features

the town's folk museum, featuring items from the lace-making trade for which Bedford was once well known. The town's most famous son is John Bunyan, author of *The Pilgrim's Progress*, which he wrote while imprisoned in the gaol. His statue stands at the top of the High Street and the Bunyan Museum in Mill Street occupies an old chapel. At nearby Elstow, where Bunyan was born, are the ruins of a convent, forming the church, and the fine 15th-century Moot Hall which houses a collection of Bunyan's works.

BISHOP'S STORTFORD

98TL4821

This busy little town has been a communications centre ever since the Roman road crossed the River Stort here. In later centuries the improvement of the Lee-Stort Navigation and the arrival of the railway fostered trade and agricultural commerce. The narrow streets that slope to the river contain contrasts in ages and styles of buildings. The old castle mound, once the property of the Bishop of London, is now a park. In South Street is the birthplace of the South African statesman, Cecil Rhodes, son of the vicar of Bishop's Stortford. Today the building houses a museum containing many of his possessions including the Bible given to him by his mother.

BUCKDEN

96TL1968

The Bishops of Lincoln had a palace at Buckden from the early Middle Ages, but now only the mellow red-brick remains of the tower, the inner gatehouse, the outer gateway and some walling survive. The Great Tower contrasts with the adjacent church which is Perpendicular in style with some fine carved details.

BURGHLEY HOUSE

96TF0406

William Cecil, Elizabeth I's great minister, created this mansion in the years up to 1587. He built on a very grand scale and the imposing façades are truly splendid. The interiors were remodelled in the late 17th century and are richly decorated. There is work by Grinling Gibbons and the main rooms are painted throughout with classical and allegorical scenes. Outside, some changes were made by Capability Brown in the 18th century. He added the Gothic Orangery as well as landscaping the park.

Bury's Angel Hill: the buildings are mostly far older than their façades suggest

BURY ST EDMUNDS

99 TL 8564

At the heart of Bury stands the great Abbey Gate and the abbey ruins; these provide a reminder of the reason for the town's existence. In medieval times pilgrims flocked to the abbey to venerate the relics of St Edmund who had been killed by the Danes in 869. The abbey was rich and ran a famous school and scriptorium in which beautiful manuscripts were produced. It also dominated the town which was re-established to the west. The main streets still follow the grid pattern laid out by Abbot Baldwin in the 11th century when he planned the town. The abbots ruled the town and most of West Suffolk until the Dissolution of the Monasteries.

Within the area of the planned town the weekly market is still held and the shopping centre thrives. The old Corn Exchange has been converted into a hall with shops below and the nearby Town Hall, or Market Cross, designed by Robert Adam in 1774, now houses an art gallery. Across the market is the Moyses Museum in a house of that name dating from the 12th century. The great space before the Abbey Gate, called Angel Hill, is bordered by elegant buildings that recall the social life conducted here by the county gentry around 1800. On the south side is the Athenaeum, a Palladian building of 1804, to the west the Angel Hotel, and in the north-west corner a Queen Anne house which now contains the Gershom Parkington Collection of Clocks and Watches.

Through the Abbey Gate lie attractive gardens round ruined fragments of the abbey. The old west arches are occupied by houses. One of the two churches in this area, St James', is now the cathedral. Its 15th-century fabric has been restored and extended and the fittings are mostly modern, superb examples of contemporary craftsmanship. The other church beside the abbey grounds is St Mary's, a fine 15th-century building with a hammerbeam roof. It contains a number of interesting monuments including one to Mary Tudor, daughter of Henry VIII.

Amongst other notable buildings in the town is the Regency Theatre Royal in Westgate Street, designed by William Wilkins in 1816.

CASTLE HEDINGHAM

99 TL 7835

A tightly packed network of little streets surrounds the church, below the wooded slopes where the castle stands. The castle was a stronghold of the de Veres, Earls of Oxford, who were powerful in this part of East Anglia. The great keep of the castle, with its 12ft-thick walls, was built around 1140 and occupied until the 16th century. Inside, the hall is a magnificent two storeys high under a fine Norman arch and contained within the thickness of the walls is a gallery. Outside, a Tudor bridge spans the dry moat.

The parish church of St Nicholas is a striking contrast of flint and brick. The 16th-century battlements and the 17th-century tower are a rich red brick but large parts of the nave and the fine east window are Norman. There are also three Norman doorways with their original doors and huge hinges. Amongst other features of interest in this church is the tomb of the 15th Earl of Oxford, standing close to the altar.

CAVENDISH

99 TL 8046

This picturesque village in the Stour Valley presents a camera-ready group of cottages with the church above the green. The houses around the green include that of Sir John Cavendish, killed in 1381 by supporters of Wat Tyler, leader of the Peasants' Revolt. Much of the church dates from the 14th century, the chancel being provided for in Cavendish's will. The Sue Ryder Foundation has its headquarters in the village, with a museum and display to explain its philanthropical work. Also in the area is the vineyard at Nether Hall

Castle Hedingham's keep stands over 100ft high. It features prominently on the town signboard

Manor, which has lectures, tours and wine tastings as well as a period house and a bygones museum to interest visitors.

CHERRY HINTON

98TL4857
Only in the 20th century has Cambridge extended its boundaries to enclose this village. The old village High Street is still recognisable as such and at its north end stands the church. This has a very fine Early English chancel. At the other end of the High Street is Cherry Hinton Hall, undistinguished itself but surrounded by pleasant recreation grounds. The Cambridge Folk Festival has been held on this site every year since 1964.

CHESTERTON

98TL4660
This suburb of Cambridge was for centuries a separate village, outside the jurisdiction of the town and, for a time, of the University as well. Consequently, it was often the scene of those activities the authorities disapproved of, like the notorious town–gown football match of 1579, before which the town lads stored weapons in the church porch for use against the scholars.

Chesterton Tower, in the vicarage garden north of the parish church, is thought to have been built as a residence for the proctor of the Canons of Vercelli, in Italy, in the mid 14th century, as nearby Chesterton Church had been given to the Vercelli canons a century earlier. The church itself has interesting medieval wall paintings over the chancel arch.

The main streets of Chesterton roll along parallel to the river, and from here one can reach the towpath. The river is sometimes alive with rowing eights as college, school and town boats practise on this stretch of water. The University 'Bumps' (see page 8) are held here in February and June.

CLARE

99TL7645
A small town with a richness of half-timbered buildings, Clare saw its greatest prosperity in the Middle Ages. Only the earthworks of the motte and bailey castle now survive, and the area has been turned into a country park with a

The turreted house known as Chesterton Tower was restored in the mid 20th century

visitor centre and a nature trail. Similarly, only ruins remain of the Augustinian priory which was founded in 1248, and these may also be seen in a garden setting. The Ancient House, near the church, dates from at least 1473 and contains the museum. The church was largely rebuilt in 1460 and like many other Suffolk churches of this period is spacious. It has some interesting wood fittings, Jacobean stalls and Tudor heraldic glass in the east window.

COCKLEY CLEY

97TF7904
This small Norfolk village houses an outdoor museum with a reconstruction of an Iron Age village, such as might have been built here by the Iceni before the Romans came. The museum also has a collection of carriages and agricultural implements and equipment. The site is overlooked by the church, which has a round tower. The ponds to the south are a breeding area for toads, and in spring people are asked to drive carefully to avoid squashing them as they cross the road.

COLNE VALLEY RAILWAY

99 TL7637

This short railway, close to Castle Hedingham, has been entirely created by the work of enthusists and is being developed as a typical rural railway of the early 1900s. Line, station and signalbox have been constructed here, and a variety of rolling stock and locomotives are on display. Refreshments are served in a veteran restaurant car. There are regular 'steaming' days with rides along the short length of track.

DENNY ABBEY

97 TL4968

Never actually an abbey, this isolated site near Waterbeach was first used by monks from Ely, then developed by the Knights Templars and finally by Franciscan nuns. The nuns' patroness was the Countess of Pembroke, foundress of Pembroke College in Cambridge. The remains comprise

On the Colne Valley Railway, Essex

the refectory, latterly a barn, and parts of the Templars' church, now incorporated in an 18th-century house.

DUXFORD

98 TL4846

The Imperial War Museum's collection at Duxford is on an old Air Force base, in operational use from World War I until 1961. Since then it has been opened to exhibit over 100 aircraft, from early biplanes to the prototype Concorde. Acquisition and restoration continue and several major flying displays take place each summer. The museum also has a flight simulator capsule, very popular with all would-be pilots. The Artillery Exhibition, military vehicles and midget submarines give a far-ranging picture of military affairs throughout this century. To broaden the picture further, and illustrate wartime housing, a 1940s prefab has been erected and furnished. It is sometimes possible to go for a flight over the airfield, and those

with their own aircraft may apply to land here.

The village of Duxford, on the other side of the motorway, has a number of charming buildings and two churches, St Peter's Church with its Norman tower, and the disused Church of St John on the village green.

Inside one of the hangars at Duxford's Imperial War Museum

ELY

97 TL5380

From miles across the Fens the great cathedral can be seen crowning the hill beside the River Ouse. This view makes the name 'Isle of Ely' intelligible, though the sea is now one of wheat, sugar beet and carrots.

In the 7th century the princess Etheldreda fled from an unwelcome marriage and took refuge here, protected by the flooded fens. She established a monastic community for both men and women and ruled it for four years. After her death (from a growth in the neck which she accepted as a punishment for her former vain love of necklaces) the monks rowed to Grantchester to find a stone coffin. Etheldreda was venerated as a saint and, despite raids by the Danes and changes made by the Normans, an abbey continued on her site until 1539, and pilgrims came to her shrine.

The remains of the monastic buildings can be seen south of the cathedral, and some are used by The King's School. The great gate or Porta still stands, and the walls of the Infirmary now form the fronts of later houses. The monastery's pretty little chapel built by Prior Crauden *c*.1324 has been cleaned and restored.

The cathedral standing today was begun around 1090 and the nave and most of the west front date from that period of Norman architecture. (It is not known exactly how or when the north

wing collapsed.) The west porch, the Galilee, was added later as is obvious from its finer columns and pointed arches. Inside, the nave stretches away between massive columns. The wooden ceiling was painted in the 19th century by devoted amateurs. At the crossing, the eye is taken swiftly upwards by the eight arches to the octagon tower, Ely's unique achievement. The Norman crossing tower had collapsed in 1322, and the monk who took on the role of architect, Alan de Walsingham, devised a new style that kept a wide open area at the heart of the cathedral,

all the figures were mutilated at the Reformation. For a time the chapel was used as a parish church.

North of the cathedral the long wall separating the precinct from the market is punctured by the Sacrist's Gate, where the Ely Museum is housed. Local history and archaeology are the main subjects covered by this museum. East of the market the road slopes down to the river, where the buildings reflect the commercial importance of the river in times past. The old Maltings was converted in 1971 to an attractive public hall. The riverside path is a pleasant place for a stroll. The west face of the cathedral looks out onto the green, bordered by the former Bishop's Palace (15th and 18th

The cathedral at Ely

works by Van Dyck, Lely and Stubbs. The park, with mock church and temple, was laid out in the 18th century and encompasses the real church, rebuilt in 1676, and dedicated to St Genevieve.

FELSTED

99 TL6720

The village is best known as the home of a public school. The first pupils, in 1564, were taught in the village guildhall, next to the church. This is still used by the school but there are extensive modern buildings. The school's founder, Lord Rich, has a handsome memorial in the parish church. Felsted Vineyards at Cricks Green (2 miles east) are open to visitors.

gradually narrowing. The octagon itself is made of wood and each pillar is 64ft high and cut from a single tree trunk. The choir dates from the 13th century and was the site of St Etheldreda's shrine until 1541. The choir stalls were made about 1342 and have fine misericords. At the east end of the cathedral are two chantry chapels built *c.*1500 and exhibiting the most ornate carving and decoration in the Perpendicular style. From the north transept a passage leads to the Lady Chapel, large and light with elaborate arcading round the walls. The sculptures told of the life and miracles of the Virgin, but

century), St Mary's Church and Cromwell House, occupied by Oliver Cromwell.

EUSTON

99 TL8978

Since around 1700 the hall at Euston has been the seat of the Dukes of Grafton. (The 3rd Duke was Chancellor of Cambridge University in the 18th century and the Grafton Centre and Fitzroy Street in Cambridge are named after him—the family name was Fitzroy.) The house contains a fine collection of paintings including

This half-timbered house at Ely has been an inn and a vicarage since it was occupied by Cromwell

Baskets of grapes ready for processing at Felsted Vineyards

FINCHINGFIELD

99TL6832

This is one of England's most picturesque villages, photographed endlessly for calendars and picture books. The stream running through the village swells to form a pond with grassy slopes on one side and on the other a succession of old-world houses, and at the top of the green the church. The 15th-century guildhall houses a collection of antiquities. North of the village are the gardens of Spains Hall, sometimes open to the public.

GODMANCHESTER

96TL2470

Godmanchester was a Roman town, situated at the crossing of the roads *Via Devana* and Ermine Street, and of more importance than Roman Cambridge. It prospered again in later centuries and a number of imposing 16th- and 17th-century houses add to the interest and variety of the street scene. One row faces straight onto the river where there is a 'Chinese' bridge originally built in 1827.

GRAFHAM WATER

96TL1568

This reservoir, created in the 1960s, has been developed for recreational use. The most prominent building is the sailing club, and there is also a residential education centre. Sailing and angling are very popular, and there are picnic and viewing areas round the lake. At its west end is a nature reserve and trail.

GRANTCHESTER

98TL4355

Forever associated with Rupert Brooke, church clocks and honey, Grantchester lies two miles south of Cambridge, far enough to be a rural haven yet within easy walking distance (see Walks, pp. 66–7). Brooke's poem is very much a personal statement for, looked at dispassionately, Grantchester is no more attractive than many other villages. It does, however, remain much as Brooke knew it, and the houses in which he lodged, The Orchard and The Old Vicarage, are still there. The church (whose clock incidentally is kept working) dates from the 14th and 15th centuries and has a chancel in the Decorated style. In the churchyard is a memorial to the dead of World War I, including Brooke.

GREAT DUNMOW

98TL6221

The curving town street, now full of shops, is a diversion of the ancient Roman road which ran westwards from Colchester. To one side are the Downs, sloping grass banks round Doctor's Pond, on which the first unsinkable lifeboat was tested in 1795. A riverside park leads northwards to the older part of Dunmow where the church stands beside the River Chelmer. The church is typical of the fine flint churches of this area.

The name of Dunmow has been associated since the Middle Ages with the award of the Dunmow Flitch. This side of bacon is on offer (once every four years) to the couple who can convince a jury that they have lived together without disagreement for a year and a day. The formalities are augmented with general festivities.

HALSTEAD

99TL8130

A steep and busy high street climbs up from the River Colne to the fine church of this small town. The notable memorials in the church are those to the 14th-century Bourchier family, who both then and since have figured prominently in the Law, the Church and literature. Four full-length figures represent the first and second lords and their wives. On the church walls are several memorials giving details of bequests of bread to be distributed to the poor of the parish—Dissenters were specifically excluded from the hand-outs!

The old brewery has a unique chapel, now turned into a museum.

Background: the lake at the centre of Hatfield Forest. Insets (left to right): the village of Finchingfield, the War Memorial at Grantchester, and the Palladian Ickworth House

HATFIELD FOREST

98TL5421

Between the village of Hatfield Broad Oak and the A120 lie the 1,000 acres of Hatfield Forest. The tracts of grass and wood are maintained by the National Trust. There are car parks within the Forest, giving easy access to the lake and the information point in the Shell House. There is also a nature reserve and a signposted nature trail.

HEMINGFORD GREY

96TL2970

This village of picturesque houses and cottages lies beside the River Ouse. The church, built of brown carstone (a type of sandstone), stands on the bank and the tower is reflected in the water. Paths lead from the village to the equally attractive Hemingford Abbots and Houghton.

HINCHINGBROOKE HOUSE

96TL2272

This 16th-century house, at one time the home of a branch of the Cromwell family, was built on the site of an 11th-century Augustinian nunnery, but is now a school. It is occasionally open to the public and the school's senior pupils are enlisted to show visitors round the house's treasures which include paintings, medieval coffins and a large collection of maps of Huntingdonshire.

HOUGHTON

96TL2871

The chief feature of this pleasant riverside village is a large 17th-century watermill which has been restored to working order. A path through the mill leads to the river and lock and on to the Hemingfords. The village houses are an attractive medley of ages and styles, many of them thatched and timber-framed.

HUNTINGDON

96TL2372

The old county of which this was the county town disappeared in 1974, absorbed into Cambridgeshire. To the Saxon town was added the customary Norman castle, of which some earthworks remain. The medieval bridge over the River Ouse also survives. A part of the Norman Hospital of St John became a grammar school in the 16th century at which both Oliver Cromwell and Samuel Pepys received some education. The building now houses the Cromwell Museum. Cromwell was born and brought up in the town and his birth is entered in the register of St John's Church (which is now kept in All Saints Church).

ICKWORTH

99TL8261

This remarkable house near the village of Horringer was the conception of Frederick Augustus Hervey, Earl of Bristol and Bishop of Derry, in 1792. A central rotunda over 100ft high is linked by curved galleries to rectangular wings. The fairly severe Palladian design is embellished with friezes on Homeric themes. Inside is the Earl-Bishop's fine collection of paintings and furniture, and the silver of his predecessors. The grounds, landscaped by Capability Brown, include a deer park and formal gardens, and provide attractive walks.

Kimbolton Castle as seen from the main entrance gateway and (above right) a carving in the entrance. Left: a plaque in the High Street

KILVERSTONE

99 TL8984
The Wildlife Park at Kilverstone specialises in animals from South America. Despite this geographical limit, a wide range of types of animal and bird can be seen, including monkeys, cats, penguins, llamas, parrots and, in particular, miniature horses. These last are no bigger than large dogs. The extensive grounds include recreation areas for children and a miniature railway.

KIMBOLTON

96 TL0967
A short but dignified main street links the church and castle. The houses are attractive with small interesting details. Kimbolton Castle is in fact a house (now used as a school) on the site of a medieval castle. Major rebuilding took place several times before Vanbrugh's early 18th-century designs resulted in the house we see today. The style is predominantly classical, and inside there are splendid wall and ceiling paintings by Pellegrini. A few traces remain of the 16th-century building in which Catherine of Aragon was detained and died.

KING'S LYNN

97 TF6220
From earliest times a port, Lynn has known periods of great prosperity, and this is reflected in the grandeur of some of the buildings. The main streets run parallel to the River Ouse and contain the chief monuments. In the 11th century the town belonged to the Bishop of Norwich and he founded a priory and the Church of St Margaret. Part of the priory hall remains and is being restored. The church has an impressive double-towered west face. Until 1741 there was a spire but this was blown down in a storm which also necessitated the rebuilding of the nave. Inside are two fine 14th-century brasses, one of which shows the 'Peacock Feast', a medieval banquet held for Edward III in 1349.

Outside the church is the Saturday Market Place, and across the road is St Margaret's House, a typical merchant's dwelling. Behind the 18th-century house at the front, the medieval warehouse stretches down to the river. Nearby is the Guildhall of the Holy Trinity, one of the medieval trade and friendly societies. Its striking chequered front, created in flint, was extended in the 19th century. This building is now the Town Hall and houses the civic treasures. Along Queen Street and to the left, by the Purfleet, stands the Customs House of 1638. It was built as an Exchange for the town's merchants but within a century had become the Customs House. The first town of Lynn did not extend north of the Purfleet brook, but the Bishop of Norwich in 1146 created another market and surrounding community. This is the Tuesday Market. Beside the square is St Nicholas Chapel, built for this northern settlement but never allowed the status of a parish church. The old Guildhall of St George in King Street has been transformed into a public meeting place and theatre, the Fermoy Centre.

LAVENHAM

99 TL9149
To walk through the centre of Lavenham is almost to return to the time of Henry VIII. The town then was at the height of its prosperity, one of the most important cloth producers of the area and therefore of England. The fortunes made went into the fine

King's Lynn: the Guildhall of the Holy Trinity, built in 1421, and a ferry crossing the River Ouse

timber houses we see today. Changes in the cloth industry, in particular the introduction of water-powered machinery, led to the decline of the industry in East Anglia and few townsmen thereafter could afford to modernise or rebuild their houses. Their loss is our gain. In recent years great, and generally successful, efforts have been made to restore these houses to their original glory. On the market-place is the original focus, the Guildhall. This was built in 1539 and now houses a museum display on the cloth trade in East Anglia. The Swan Inn also occupies a handsome set of buildings including the old Wool Hall. Nearby is the Priory, a

Tudor house recently rescued and restored so that the timbering and Elizabethan wall paintings may be seen. It also has a herb garden. The Little Hall, which contains a fine arts collection, is the headquarters of the Suffolk Preservation Society. As in other wool towns, the prosperity found its greatest expression in the church. The Earls of Oxford were the major promoters of the rebuilding here, together with the Spring family, the leading merchants in the town. The massive square tower, which bears no less than 32 examples of the Spring family's coat of arms, tops the hill beside the long 15th-

The Guildhall at Lavenham

century nave and the 14th-century chancel. The large windows make it light and airy within. There is fine detail in the carving of the side chapels, all from the early 16th century.

LINTON

98TL5646

Bypassed by the main road, this village can now enjoy its attractive High Street in peace. A number of old houses and cottages create a picturesque street scene. North of the village is Chilford Hall with its vineyard, which is open to summer visitors. South of the village is Linton Zoo, a family-run collection which has achieved some successful breeding of a number of rare animals including the Indian eagle owl and the binturong, a long-haired, fruit-eating Asian mammal. A variety of mammals, birds and reptiles live in the well-maintained gardens.

LODE WATERMILL

98TL5362

Although situated in the hamlet of Lode, the watermill is reached through the grounds of Anglesey Abbey (see page 70). The mill, now restored to working order, stands where Quy (pronounced to rhyme with 'why') Water becomes Bottisham Lode, an artificial channel cut originally by the Romans.

LONG MELFORD

99 TL 8646

The 'Long' of this village's name is, indeed, descriptive. The houses are strung out along the Bury to Sudbury road, and there are few side streets. At the upper end a large green lies at the junction with the Clare road. It is crowned by the church, one of the famous 'wool' churches built on the proceeds of that trade in the 15th century. The chief benefactors were the Cloptons, lords of the manor of Kentwell. They built their own chapel in the church. The church is in the Perpendicular style, with fine flintwork on the outside and lofty arcades inside. Near the church is a handsome set of almshouses built in the 16th century.

North of the church, at the end of an avenue of limes ¾ mile long, stands Kentwell Hall. The present house was built *c.*1560 and is a fine specimen of the brick mansions of the time, having two wings at right-angles to the hall range. Behind stands the old medieval hall. Both are contained by a moat and gardens. For three weeks each summer Kentwell Hall reverts to the 16th century to show schoolchildren and adults what life was like under the Tudors.

Nearer the heart of the village stands Melford Hall, built by Sir William Cordell around 1570. A pretty octagonal gazebo tops the boundary wall. The house, of red brick, is typical of its date. Amongst other items, it contains paintings and navigational instruments illustrating the naval careers of the Parkers, who owned the hall from 1786.

The main street is full of charming houses, many 16th century. The Bull Inn is one of the finest. There are also a number of antique shops in the village.

LONGTHORPE TOWER

96 TL 1698

On the outskirts of Peterborough stands Longthorpe Tower, part of a manor house dating from around 1300. The main room contains a set of medieval wall paintings hardly paralleled elsewhere. They were uncovered in the 1940s and show typical themes such as the Seven Ages of Man, the Nativity, King David, and the Wheel of the Five Senses. Although rather faded, they are a reminder of what most churches and great houses must have looked like in the Middle Ages.

MADINGLEY

98 TL 3960

This tiny village west of Cambridge is situated on the edge of the park of Madingley Hall, a 16th-century house owned by Cambridge University and used as a residential centre and base by the Board of Extra-Mural Studies.

On a slope outside the village are the graves of the American Military Cemetery. A lofty chapel and the Wall of Remembrance stand beside a pool overlooking the ranks of white crosses and memorials to Americans based in East Anglia who died in World War II.

MARCH

97 TL 4197

When the railways were built this market town became a main junction. Up to that time it was a modest Fen settlement. The original centre was well south of the River Nene, where the church of St Wendreda stands. This local saint was honoured with a church ceiling of the utmost splendour. Some 118 angels in three tiers are poised above the worshippers. The town centre shifted in later years to the riverside where there is a market and the principal buildings. The town museum, with displays of domestic and agricultural artefacts, and photographs and documents relating to the March area, is in the High Street.

MILDENHALL

97 TL 7074

The name of Mildenhall is now associated with the Air Force bases in this area, but the town itself has a long history. In the market-place still stand the pump and the market cross (an umbrella-like wooden structure). The church is very fine. It is built largely in the Perpendicular style, with a roof richly decorated with carved angels. The memorials include one to Sir Henry North portraying himself and his wife and six children. There is a small town museum near the market. Part of Thetford Forest lies east of the town and there are picnic areas beside the main road.

Engines and enthusiasts at the Nene Valley Railway Museum, near Peterborough

NENE VALLEY RAILWAY

96TL0799
This restored steam railway has its base at Wansford on the A1. There is a collection of 18 steam locomotives, with diesel engines, carriages and wagons, and a museum and exhibition. The railway runs for 7½ miles through the Nene Valley Park to Peterborough, stopping at three stations *en route*. The line is often used as a film set but, those occasions apart, there are regular rides for visitors throughout the summer.

NEWMARKET

98TL6463
The essence of Newmarket is horse-racing. When James I set up a hunting lodge here around 1610, there was no more than a very small market town (which had been 'new' in the early Middle Ages). The Stuart kings enjoyed the open

Training the racehorses at Newmarket. At the Horse-Racing Museum in the town exhibits include these sets of jockey's colours

gallops possible on the heaths outside the town, and from the time of the first race for a gold cup in 1634, racing has continued. The National Horse-Racing Museum in the High Street tells the story. The Jockey Club also has its base in the High Street. The two racecourses are used for different meetings, but even when no event is taking place

strings of horses can be seen walking from their stables and galloping on the heath.

NORTON

99TL9565
The Tropical Bird Gardens in Norton cover four acres and contain over 100 species of foreign birds and waterfowl. The tropical house and aviaries are planted to create natural conditions for the birds.

OLD WARDEN

96TL1343
In this pleasant quiet village, where in the last century the Shuttleworth family produced steam farm machinery, there is now a unique collection of veteran aeroplanes and road vehicles. The aircraft are all airworthy and regular flying displays are held. The hangars are close to the family's Victorian house and garden, and the runways are grass; thus the atmosphere of early aviation prevails.

Elizabethan Melford Hall, now a National Trust property

OXBOROUGH

97 TF 7401

The small village is dominated by lovely Oxburgh Hall, built around 1482. It is in red brick within a moat. Although some parts were taken down or altered in the 18th and 19th centuries, enough remains to give the flavour of the late Middle Ages. In the tower rooms are furnishings and treasures, including embroideries worked by Mary Queen of Scots and her keeper, the Countess of Shrewsbury. A chapel was added to the house by Pugin in the 19th century.

Outside the Hall is the parish church, a melancholy remnant of the much larger building destroyed when the tower collapsed in 1948. Only the north wall of the nave remains, the chancel being used for worship. The Bedingfield Chapel, created by the owners of the Hall, was undamaged and contains remarkable monuments in terracotta, made about 1500.

PEAKIRK

96 TF 1606

The water gardens at Peakirk are maintained by the Wildfowl Trust for the support of 112 species of birds, including flamingos and exotic geese and swans. There are also areas of wood, exhibitions and other facilities for visitors.

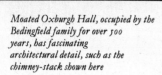

Moated Oxburgh Hall, occupied by the Bedingfield family for over 500 years, has fascinating architectural detail, such as the chimney-stack shown here

PETERBOROUGH

96 TL 1999

Over the last 20 years Peterborough has expanded enormously to house 'London overspill', but at its heart there is still the cathedral from which it takes its name. This began as an abbey and gave rise to the town in the Saxon period. The usual market grew up in front of the abbey gate. The old Guildhall, built in 1671, marks the place. There are few historic buildings in the city but it is a very lively place. A new indoor shopping centre has been added to the old shopping and market areas, and has won much praise for its design as well as support from the region's shoppers. Between the new Queensgate shopping centre and the river are a stadium, swimming pools and the Key Theatre. There are other major sports facilities on the north side of Peterborough and in the Nene Valley Park.

Peterborough Cathedral stands facing the city centre in a precinct containing some remnants of the medieval abbey. The Great Gate dates from about the 13th century and leads to the cathedral west

The triple-arched west front of Peterborough Cathedral, built of local Barnack stone

front, composed of three lofty arches. Inside, most of the chancel and nave are in the Norman style, solid and plain, from the 12th century. The painted wooden ceiling of the nave is an important work from about 1220. Round the choir are many memorials to the abbots, and the Monk's Stone of *c*.800. The notably different part is the extreme east end, which has a beautiful fan vault from *c*.1500. Two queens were buried at Peterborough, Catherine of Aragon, Henry VIII's first and rejected wife, and Mary Queen of Scots who was executed at Fotheringhay. Between these two events the abbey was dissolved and the Bishopric of Peterborough created. Most of the monks' buildings were demolished or converted. As a reminder of the monks' work, a herb garden has been created on the site of the cloisters.

Reaching out westwards from the city are the Ferry Meadows, part of a much longer stretch of open country, the Nene Valley Park. Set in acres of grassland are sporting facilities, including a water-sports centre, and wildlife areas. Through the park runs the Nene Valley Railway (see page 81). Many important and fascinating sites have been found along the Nene Valley by archaeologists. There have been finds from the Iron Age and many more from the Roman period when there were important industrial sites in this area. Some of the finds are displayed in the City Museum in Priestgate which also houses an art gallery.

REACH

97 TL5666

The works of the Romans and the Saxons meet at this tiny fenland village. From the River Cam a channel originally cut by the Romans stretches eastward. At Reach it meets the west end of the Devil's Dyke, a massive earthwork designed to keep out invaders who might be coming along the Icknield Way. The Dyke extends for over 7 miles and can be walked all the way. Nowadays it is also managed to maintain its botanical interest. Reach itself was the site of an historic annual fair, belonging to the Cambridge Corporation. The ceremony is still observed on the May Day Bank Holiday, with some modest celebrations.

ROYSTON

98 TL3541

At the crossing of ancient ways at the foot of the hill, this town was created. A priory was founded in the 12th century and the canons were given the right to hold a market. The old Roman road widened out in the town to form a long market-place running north–south. Houses now fill the open space but two parallel roads remain, one with the old inn archways and yards. The priory church was bought by the townspeople in 1539 to become the parish church, then thoroughly restored by the Victorians. Beside and beneath the main street is a cave in the chalk which it is believed was used by the Knights Templars in the Middle Ages. With its medieval carvings, it was rediscovered in 1742. The town museum in Lower King Street has good local history exhibits.

SAFFRON WALDEN

98 TL5438

Walden is set in a valley, a contrast to the Cambridgeshire towns to the north. 'Saffron' comes from the saffron crocus, an important crop plant of the area in the days when it was used for dyeing. This very attractive town has picturesque views along streets with houses of different ages. Particularly notable is the pargetting or ornamental plasterwork on houses in Church Street. The Youth Hostel in Bridge Street is another fine medieval house. Nearby are the Bridge End Gardens, laid out in the 19th century and recently restored to their original splendour.

The fine church spire with its flying buttresses can be seen from a distance, and it surmounts a church of equal elegance. Most of the church was rebuilt *c*.1500 in the Perpendicular style and its architect was John Wastell, Master Mason of King's College Chapel. The Audley family, builders of Audley End, have a vault here. Near the church stands the museum, in what was once the castle bailey. It has a local history display, together with natural history and ceramics collections. Outside are the ruins of the old castle keep, now only flint and rubble. The common stretches east of the interesting market-place and at its far end is an ancient turf-cut maze, possibly a pre-Christian relic.

Pargetting in Saffron Walden

ST IVES

96TL3171
Lying beside the River Great Ouse, with other streams and flooded gravel pits round, St Ives is a boating centre as well as a market town. Nowadays the boating is recreational; formerly it was commercial. The old approach to the town was across the medieval bridge, which still has its little chapel. This leads to the market street with the statue of Oliver Cromwell, a former resident. The town takes its name from St Ivo, a Persian bishop whose body, supposedly, was found here around 1000, several hundred years after his death. A priory was built on the site and was granted the right to hold a market and fairs. At the western end of the main street stands the 15th-century parish church, overlooking a pleasant riverside area called The Waits. Nearby is the Norris Museum which houses local antiquities.

ST NEOTS

96TL1860
The little village of Eynesbury was the original settlement, before a priory was founded in the 10th century. The monks had abstracted the body of St Neot from a Cornish grave, to become the focus of their worship. Nothing now remains of the priory but the name. The town, however, flourishes. Between the Hen Brook and the priory site is the large market square with some elegant 18th-century merchants' houses, and just south of the High Street is the parish church. This is a magnificent building of the 15th century. Across the river the meadows have been laid out as a large park.

SANDY

96TL1649
Market gardening and light industry are the chief occupations in Sandy, a pleasant town on the River Ivel. On the wooded hills that rise east of the town is the headquarters of the Royal Society for the Protection of Birds (RSPB). The Society also has a reserve at Sandy of over 100 acres where wild birds attracted by the gardens, woodland and heath may be observed—and there is a nature trail.

SAWSTON

98TL4849
Now a large and busy village, the old core of Sawston still has period charm. The former focus of the village, the Hall, was rebuilt in the reign of Queen Mary, after her enemies had destroyed its predecessor. The Huddleston family lived here until the 1970s. It is now an educational centre. The adjacent church has an attractive mixture of styles and a number of (wall-mounted) memorial brasses.

The village college, at the far end of Sawston, was the first to be set up by the pioneering education officer Henry Morris. Their purpose—apart from providing 11 to 18 year-olds with an

The RSPB headquarters at Sandy

education—is to serve as a learning and social centre for the whole community. Village colleges also differ from other schools in that they are federated.

SHEPRETH

98TL3947
This quiet village is typical of the Cam Valley. Between here and neighbouring Barrington (noted for its large village green) is a designated riverside walk. In the village is a fish farm and animal sanctuary, where a variety of domestic and foreign birds and animals can be seen.

STAMFORD

96TF0207
After the brick of Cambridgeshire, the stone buildings of Stamford, just in Lincolnshire, are a surprise. They give an extra elegance to a fine town. The southern approach, past St Martin's Church, is particularly impressive. The 15th-century church contains memorials to the Cecil family of Burghley House (see page 71). The town also has four other medieval churches, each with interesting details. Browne's Hospital is another important 15th-century building, founded as a set of almshouses with a chapel and rooms round a central court. There are few remains of the religious houses, but the George Hotel, next to the bridge, claims the crypt of the medieval hostel run by the Knights of St John. The hotel is now well known for open-air performances of Shakespeare's plays.

STANSTED MOUNTFITCHET

98TL5124
Now best known for its international airport, the town of Stansted has a long history and a charm imparted by its old houses and hilly narrow streets. A restored windmill stands above all.

The earthworks of the Norman castle, the work of the Duke of Boulougne shortly after the Norman Conquest, have been surmounted by a reconstruction of the timber buildings and palisades that might have existed around 1100. With models, artefacts and real domestic animals, life in a Norman baron's house is vividly recreated. Richard de Montfichet, who gave his name to the town,

of East Anglia's industrial heritage. There are also steam traction engines, a gypsy camp and the museum's live exhibit, a Suffolk Punch horse called Remus. Craft, steam and working horse demonstrations take place from March to October.

The town itself has some of the marks of earlier commercial development, including the canalised river.

Stansted Mountfitchet: the windmill, and the stocks at the castle

The Boby Building at Stowmarket

was the last owner of the castle, which was attacked and destroyed as a result of the Baron's opposition to King John.

STILTON

96TL1689

The name of this village is known far and wide, but it was not here that the famous cheese was made. Rather, this was a transmission point on the Old North Road on the journey from Leicestershire. Although the village is bypassed by modern main roads, the old inns still stand in the High Street and, of course, Stilton cheese is on offer.

STOWMARKET

99TM0458

This agricultural market town is probably the ideal setting for the Museum of East Anglian Life. The museum grounds extend from close to the market to the river and display a variety of aspects of past rural life. Several buildings have been reconstructed here, including a watermill, a wind-pump and a smithy. The largest structure on the site, the Boby Building, is an 1870s engineering workshop housing craftsmen, a steam gallery, a bioscope show and an exhibition

The Engine House at Stretham contains one of the few surviving beam pumping engines

STRETHAM

97TL5174
The village stands at the end of a slight ridge, above the Old West River. On the river itself stands the three-storey pumping house containing the Stretham Beam Engine, built in 1831 to lift water from the drained fields up into the river. Beside the engine is a collection of objects and curiosities from the local fens.

SUDBURY

99TL8741
This town has many reminders of its long and interesting history. The River Stour, on which it lies, was once navigable to the sea, and Sudbury was a port with quays and warehouses. Weaving was its great trade and silk weaving is still carried on here. Some old cottages with their large upstairs windows to light the looms can still be seen.

The painter Gainsborough (1727–88) is the town's most famous son. His birthplace is now the Gainsborough Museum, with furniture of his time and his own and other artists' paintings. The house itself was built in the 15th century and modernised by Gainsborough's father.

The earliest church was St Gregory's, greatly enlarged by Simon of Sudbury in the 15th century to accommodate a college of priests. Simon became Archbishop of Canterbury but he antagonised the poor and was killed by the rebels during the Peasants' Revolt of 1381. His head was returned to the church. When the college of priests was abolished at the Reformation, St Peter's, on

Market Hill, became the parish church. It dates chiefly from the 15th century, as does All Saints' Church near the site of the old priory.

SWAFFHAM

97TF8109
The centre of this market town is dignified by an elegant 'cross' of 1783, in the form of a rotunda topped by Ceres the goddess of the harvest. The corn hall built in 1858 is not so elegant. There are several handsome buildings in the main streets but the church is particularly fine. It is mostly 15th century, with a double hammerbeam roof adorned with angels. There is a memorial to Oliver Cromwell's grandmother and the ministers' stalls have carved figures. On one is represented the Pedlar of Swaffham. The story says that the pedlar dreamt of finding treasure in London. On reaching the city he met a man who had dreamt of finding gold in a garden in Swaffham, Norfolk. The pedlar rushed home and indeed dug up a pot of treasure in his own garden.

This tale has become linked with the real John Chapman, a benefactor of the church in the 15th century.

THAXTED

98TL6131
It was the cutlery trade in the 14th and 15th centuries that made Thaxted a prosperous town. The resultant wealth went particularly into the church, the spire of which can be seen from miles away. It tops a large spacious interior in the Perpendicular style. Major rebuilding began in 1340 and was finished in 1510. There is fine work in the wooden ceilings, and a number of interesting fittings including an unusual oak font cover. Narrow lanes lead from the south of the churchyard to the Guildhall, facing down Town Street.

The Guildhall was built by the Cutlers' Guild in the 15th century and has since been used as a town hall and as a school. Its open ground floor was originally for market use, but one corner now contains the 18th-century lock-up. The trade that saw the erection of the fine medieval houses declined in Tudor times, but a variety of later buildings add to the picturesque appearance of Town Street. Every summer the whole town comes alive during the annual visit of the Morris Ring, the national association of morris dancers.

John Webb's windmill nearby houses a collection of rural bygones and an 1835 fire engine.

THETFORD

99TL8783
Over the last 30 years this town has deliberately expanded and introduced new industries. At its heart there are reminders of a past that goes back to Saxon times. To one side is the castle mound, now an open space, and on the other the ruins of the priory, where the Dukes of Norfolk were buried in the Middle Ages. A 15th-century half-timbered building, the Ancient House, contains the town museum with displays including Stone Age implements from the surrounding Breckland. The town's most famous native, Thomas Paine, left Thetford to champion human rights in the American and French Revolutions. He is commemorated

Sign showing the Pedlar of Swaffham

in the town by a fine statue. There are several more buildings of interest around the compact shopping centre and by the Rivers Thet and Little Ouse which meet here.

THORNEY

96TF2804
At this remote site in the Fens stood Thorney Abbey. It was begun in the 10th century and the portion that remains is early 11th century. After the Dissolution of the Monasteries, the village and estate went to the Earls (later Dukes) of Bedford who had so much to do with the draining of the Fens. Most of the nave of the abbey became the parish church in 1638. Round the grass square that now represents the cloisters are fine 17th- to 18th-century houses. Along the main road are the white brick estate houses built in the 19th century by the then Duke.

TRUMPINGTON

98TL4455
Now a suburb of Cambridge, this village has been mentioned by the poets since Chaucer. A few older buildings stand west of the

A quiet stroll in Thetford Forest, situated north-west of the town

Cambridge road, on the way to the river and Grantchester. The church, built mostly in the 14th century, contains a life-size memorial brass to Sir Roger de Trumpington, one of the earliest brasses in the country.

WANDLEBURY RING

98TL4953
The generally flat nature of Cambridge encourages humorous references to Wandlebury and the Gog Magog Hills as the Alps of Cambridge. Their maximum height, however, is only about 250ft. The focal point of interest is the circular earthwork, the remains

Sir Roger de Trumpington's brass, the second oldest in England

of an Iron Age fort, in the centre of which a mansion was built in the 18th century. All that now remains of this is the stable block, beneath which is marked the grave of the Godolphin Arab, ancestor of many English racehorses, which died in 1753. The estate belongs to the Cambridge Preservation Society, which maintains the woods and 13 acres of open grass for public use. A nature trail is marked out, and paths lead to a section of the old Roman road to Cambridge, now a track.

Inset: the ruins of Thetford Priory

The Brinks at Wisbech, a pair of streets either side of the river

WEETING

97 TL7788
Near Weeting are some of the oldest monuments in East Anglia. Three miles north-east of the village lie Grimes Graves, Neolithic flint mines. An area between the modern pine forests presents a pock-marked slope, where the ancient pits have collapsed in on themselves. Several have been excavated and one is kept open for visitors to inspect.

At the village of Weeting stand the remains of the 12th-century manor house, within a moat. Next door is the church which has a Victorian round tower.

The largest area of Thetford Forest lies east of here. Visitors are allowed to walk through the woods, planted mostly with conifers, and there are areas for picnicking.

WELNEY

97 TL5294
Between the two great drainage channels of the Fens, the Old and New Bedford Rivers, are the Ouse Washes, wetland that is attractive to vast numbers of waterfowl. At Welney the Wildfowl Trust maintains hides and an observatory used by both scientists and amateur birdwatchers.

The Whittlesey Straw Bear

WEST STOW

99 TL8170
The country park 4 miles west of Bury St Edmunds has, besides its picnic areas and walks, a unique reconstruction of an Anglo-Saxon village. Archaeologists worked on this site for several years, discovering the nature of the wooden buildings and their construction, and, using this knowledge, have built five replicas.

WHITTLESEY

96 TL2797
Surrounded by the wide stretches of fen and the long straight drainage ditches, Whittlesey stands in a world quite different from southern Cambridgeshire. A number of pleasant buildings cluster round the market-place with its distinctive Butter Cross. There is a small local museum. St Mary's Church has a particularly fine spire; St Andrew's is more modest but still attractive. The old custom of parading the Straw Bear, a man bedecked by straw, has been revived and takes place in January.

WICKEN FEN

97 TL5770
Next to the village of Wicken a last piece of natural fen is being preserved by the National Trust. While efficient drainage has converted the surrounding country into productive farmland, the water level at Wicken is maintained artificially high in order to preserve the scrub and sedge that used to cover this area. The associated bird and insect life can also be observed on the reserve. Marked walks may be taken round the Fen and there is an interesting information display.

WIDDINGTON

98 TL5331
In the village of Widdington stands Priors Hall Barn, a recently restored medieval building. To the east is Mole Hall Wildlife Park. Mole Hall itself is a half-timbered manor house surrounded by a moat in which some of the wildfowl swim. In the gardens and paddocks are primates, otters, wallabies, deer and other mammals. There is also a butterfly pavilion with British and exotic butterflies and other insects.

WIMPOLE HALL

98 TL3351
The house, park and farm at Wimpole were left to the National Trust after the death of the last owner and occupant, Mrs Elsie Bambridge, daughter of Rudyard Kipling. The house as it stands was constructed chiefly in the 18th century. The imposing south front is a composite creation. James Gibbs was responsible for some of the work, including the fine library and the chapel. Sir John Soane designed the Yellow Drawing Room and the unusual plunge bath. During the same period the gardens were being landscaped, first by Capability Brown around 1770, and then by Humphry Repton in the early 1800s. A double avenue of elms once stretched 2 miles southwards but fell to Dutch Elm Disease. It is now being replanted. North of the house the features include a large Gothic folly and a Chinese bridge. Beside the house is the church, partly medieval, partly 18th century, which contains several attractive monuments.

The scattered houses that constituted the village were removed in the formation of the

The South Drawing Room at Wimpole Hall featuring painted furniture from South Germany

park and estate houses can be seen along the main road.

The Home Farm is a centre for rare breeds and uses the original farm buildings, including the great barn, designed by Soane. In the barn is a collection of old farm vehicles and implements to illustrate the methods of farming before mechanisation. Animals to be seen include sheep, goats, Tamworth pigs, longhorn cattle and varieties of domestic fowl. The stables, designed by Kendall in 1851, are currently being restored.

WISBECH

97 TF 4609
Set in the heart of the fenland, Wisbech has a surprising number of elegant Georgian houses, a sign of the prosperity that came to the area after the draining of the Fens and improvements to the river channel. Wisbech is still a port. The most famous views are of the houses on The Brinks, the streets

facing the River Nene where it flows through the centre of the town. Each house is different, yet they form a harmonious and very attractive whole. Of particular note is Peckover House, owned by the National Trust. Built about 1722, the dignified exterior conceals an interior with richly decorated overmantels in panelled rooms, all from the early and mid 18th century. The garden has a Victorian layout with several interesting specimen trees including one of the largest maidenhair (gingko) trees in Britain.

Where the market area meets The Brinks stands a memorial (by George Gilbert Scott) to Thomas Clarkson, a native of Wisbech who campaigned ardently to abolish the slave trade. East of this lies The Crescent, a more uniform 18th-century range which marks the outer edge of the medieval castle site. The centre is occupied by the fine Castle Lodge of 1816. In the small square beyond is the purpose-built museum of 1846. Exhibits on display include a range of objects and photographs from the area and a collection of ceramics. East again

stands the church. It is dominated by a tower set on the north-west side and is unusually wide, having a double nave. The building dates chiefly from the 14th century.

The theatre built in Alexandra Road in 1793 has been largely destroyed by subsequent users, but is once again a centre for drama and the arts.

Gibbs' chapel at Wimpole Hall dates from 1719 and contains paintings by Sir James Thornhill

MAPS & DRIVES

*Historic aircraft and military vehicles can be seen at the
Imperial War Museum at Duxford Airfield, former Battle
of Britain fighter station*

The Cambridgeshire, Suffolk and Essex borders

Heading eastwards from Cambridge this drive first visits the house and gardens at Anglesey Abbey then continues towards Newmarket where the area's associations with horse-racing are apparent. From here the route heads south-west to Saffron Walden and Audley End House, passing through several attractive villages, and returns along the Cam valley.

From Cambridge follow signs for Newmarket to leave by the A1303. After a couple of miles the road passes Cambridge Airport. Two miles further on, at the A45 roundabout, take the second exit, then branch left on to the B1102, signed Burwell. Pass through Stow cum Quy and continue across the low-lying countryside to reach **Anglesey Abbey**. This National Trust property has 13th-century monastic origins and was remodelled in about 1600.

At the cross-roads ¼ mile beyond the house, turn right on to an unclassified road, signed Bottisham. About ¾ mile beyond the village of Bottisham turn left on to the A1303, signed Newmarket. In 1¾ miles cross the Newmarket Bypass and continue to the roundabout 2¼ miles further on. Take the second exit, the A1304, passing the turning to the National Stud (on the left). The famous Newmarket Heath with its two racecourses is then crossed to reach the outskirts of **Newmarket** *in Suffolk. On entering the built-up district the main tour turns right on to the B1061, signed Haverhill.* (Alternatively keep forward to visit the handsome town centre and the National Horse-Racing Museum, then retrace your route to this junction to rejoin the tour.)

Leaving Newmarket the B1061 shortly bears right and passes over a level-crossing to re-enter Cambridgeshire. After a mile or so the road crosses the Devil's Dyke—a 7th-century earthwork some 7¼ miles long (see under **Reach**). *Continue through Dullingham and 1 mile beyond the village take the B1052, signed Linton. At Brinkley bear left then right. Continue through Weston Colville, turn left after ½ mile, and continue to West Wratting then Balsham. Here bear right and at the far end of the village keep left. Three miles further on the picturesque village of* **Linton** *is reached. At the T-junction turn right, signed Hadstock, and proceed along the main street. Cross the River Granta and shortly turn left on to the A604, then take the next turning right, the B1052, signed Saffron Walden.* To the right is **Linton Zoo** which displays a wide variety of wildlife in 10 acres of landscaped enclosures.

Remain on the B1052 and at Hadstock bear right. Continue through Little Walden before entering the delightful town of **Saffron Walden** *which retains many old attractive houses.* There are slight remains of a 12th-century castle near to the interesting local museum, and on the Common there is a maze. The fine 15th-century church has a lofty spire, added in 1831.

In Saffron Walden, turn left (one-way) then shortly right, following the Bishop's Stortford signs. On reaching the War Memorial keep left and ¼ mile further on take the unclassified road, signed Audley End. After ¾ mile the splendid 17th-century mansion of **Audley End House**, *set in very attractive parkland, can be seen to the right.*

In ¼ mile, at the T-junction, turn right on to the B1383, signed Cambridge. The drive now heads northwards following the valley of the River Cam, passing through Littlebury and on to Great Chesterford. Here take the unclassified road, signed Duxford, and pass under a railway bridge then the M11 Motorway. At Ickleton turn left (no sign) and at the far end of the village bear right (signed Duxford). In 1¼ miles bear right again, passing the Plough public house, to enter **Duxford**. *At the church turn left, signed Whittlesford, and after ¾ mile the road reaches the junction with the A505. From here a short detour can be made by turning left to visit the Imperial War Museum's collection of aircraft and vehicles at* **Duxford Airfield**.

The main drive turns right then immediately left across the A505 to continue along the unclassified road through Whittlesford. *At the next village, Little Shelford, turn right at the church. Shortly afterwards cross the River Cam and keep forward (signed Cambridge) into Great Shelford. Here turn left, A1301, and follow the main road to* **Trumpington**. *At the traffic signals turn right then immediately left unclassified signed Grantchester. In ¼ mile turn left again in order to make a diversion to the pretty village of* **Grantchester**. *At the Rupert Brooke public house keep right, then in 1¼ miles turn right on to the A603 (no sign) for the return to Cambridge.*

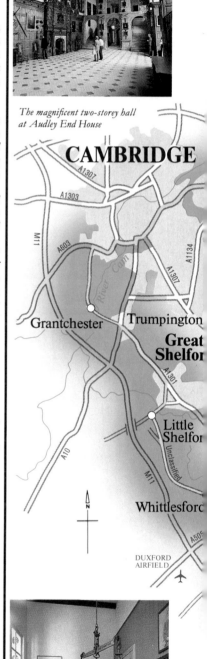

The magnificent two-storey hall at Audley End House

'The Weighing Room' on display at the National Museum of Horse-Racing, Newmarket

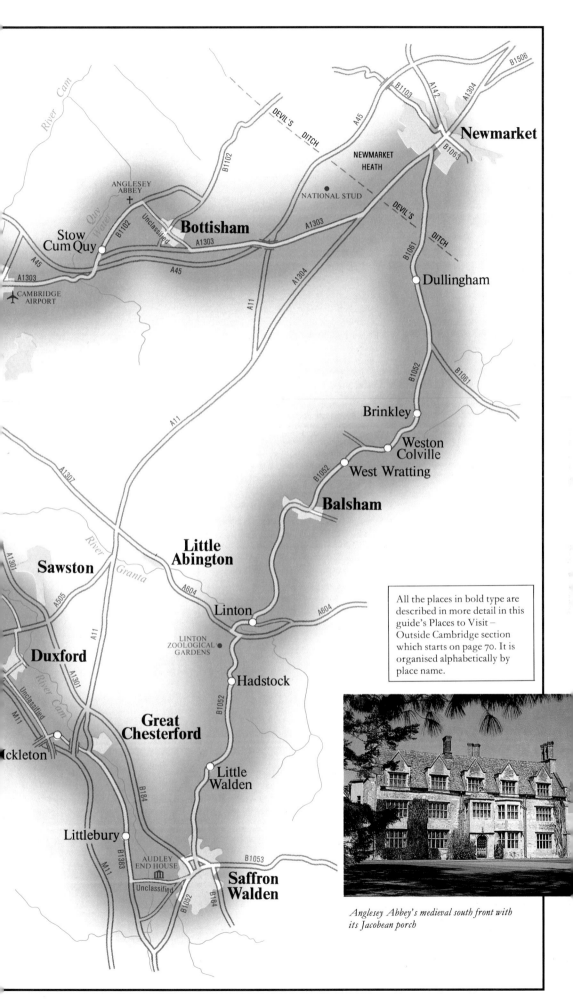

River Cam

B1506

Newmarket

DEVIL'S DITCH

B1103

A142

A1304

B1063

A45

NEWMARKET HEATH

B1102

ANGLESEY ABBEY ✝

Quy Water

NATIONAL STUD

DEVIL'S DITCH

Unclassified

B1102

Bottisham

A1303

A1303

B1061

Stow Cum Quy

A45

A1304

Dullingham

A1303

CAMBRIDGE AIRPORT ✈

A11

B1052

B1061

Brinkley

A11

Weston Colville

B1052

West Wratting

Balsham

A1307

River Granta

Little Abington

Sawston

A604

A604

A505

Linton

A11

LINTON ZOOLOGICAL GARDENS

Duxford

A1301

River Cam

Hadstock

Unclassified

M11

B1052

Great Chesterford

All the places in bold type are described in more detail in this guide's Places to Visit – Outside Cambridge section which starts on page 70. It is organised alphabetically by place name.

ckleton

Little Walden

Littlebury

B1383

M11

AUDLEY END HOUSE 🏛

B1053

Unclassified

Saffron Walden

B1052

B184

Anglesey Abbey's medieval south front with its Jacobean porch

History along the River Ouse

The Wall of Remembrance at the American Military Cemetery, Madingley

This drive to the west of Cambridge takes in the historically fascinating towns of St Ives, Godmanchester, Huntingdon and St Neots—all attractively set beside the Ouse—as well as a number of picturesque villages with interesting associations, and peaceful, open countryside.

From Cambridge follow signs for Bedford (A45) to leave by the A1303 Madingley Road. In 1½ miles cross the M11 and 1 mile further on pass the American Military Cemetery (on the right). At the next roundabout take the third exit on to an unclassified road for the attractive village of **Madingley***. Continue forward to the A604 and turn left to follow the dual-carriageway road. Nearly 2 miles further on branch left on to the B1050, signed Chatteris, and at the roundabout turn right to cross the A604. Continue on the B1050 to the edge of Longstanton then turn left for Willingham. Here keep forward on the Earith/St Ives road, shortly passing an interesting old church. In 2 miles follow the River Great Ouse and later turn left on to the A1123, signed Huntingdon, then cross the river bridges into Earith. Proceed to Needingworth and in 1¼ miles, at the roundabout, follow the signs to enter the town centre of* **St Ives***. At the west end of the town is the 15th-century church with its tall spire. There is also a town museum and a rare bridge chapel.*

Follow signs for Cambridge and cross the river again. Shortly turn right on to an unclassified road, signed The Hemingfords, for **Hemingford Grey***. Keep forward into the village (signed The River), then turn left into Braggs Lane, signed Hemingford Abbots. Shortly turn right into Manor Road for this equally picturesque village, where the church has a fine spire. Here turn left, signed Huntingdon, then in ¾ mile cross the road bridge and join the A604. One mile further on branch left (still following signs for Huntingdon, B1043) and at the roundabout take the third exit on to an unclassified road for* **Godmanchester***. This former Roman town has some Georgian and older, timbered houses, an Elizabethan grammar school and a 15th-century church with fine interior details.*

From Godmanchester branch right, B1043, and cross the River Great Ouse by a 14th-century bridge for the historic town of **Huntingdon***. The town hall dates from 1745, and there are many Georgian houses, one of which was occupied by the poet Cowper. The former grammar school is now a Cromwell museum.*

From the Ring Road (one-way system) follow signs for Kettering (A604) to leave by the A141. Half a mile further on, to the right of the road, lies **Hinchingbrooke House***. In another ¼ mile, at the roundabout, turn left (signed London) into Brampton. Two miles further on join the A1, and shortly take the second turning left on to an unclassified road into* **Buckden***. Buckden Palace, the remains of the former residence of the Bishops of Lincoln, is also famous as one of the houses where Catherine of Aragon was imprisoned.*

At the end of the village, at the roundabout, take the second exit on to the B661, signed Kimbolton. The drive then passes **Grafham Water Reservoir***, created in the 1960s, with its picnic areas. Continue through Perry, then at Great Staughton turn left on to the St Neots road, A45. Later skirt Hail Weston and cross the A1. Join the B1048 then in ¾ mile turn left and cross the River Great Ouse to enter* **St Neots***. The town has a wide market-place and a 15th-century parish church with a fine carved tower.*

At the end of the High Street turn right on to the B1043, signed Little Barford. In 1 mile, at the roundabout, take the first exit (signed The Gransdens, B1046) then take the next turning right into Potton Road, B1046. One mile further on bear left and proceed to Abbotsley. Continue along the B1046 and in 1½ miles turn right then immediately left for Great Gransden. Pass the Crown and Cushion public house and turn left (unclassified, signed Industrial Estate), then at the roundabout turn left again, signed Caxton. At Caxton turn right then left across the A14, signed Toft and Bourn. Shortly to the left is Bourn Windmill, a post-mill dating from 1636.

In 1 mile, at the T-junction, turn right and enter Bourn. Follow the Toft/Cambridge road and at the far end of the village join the B1046. Continue through Toft and Comberton to Barton, then in ½ mile turn left on to the A603. Cross the M11 and at the roundabout take the third main exit on to an unclassified road for the attractive village of **Grantchester***. Here, turn right (signed Trumpington), and cross the River Cam to reach* **Trumpington***. At the War Memorial turn left on to the A1309 (no sign) for the return to Cambridge.*

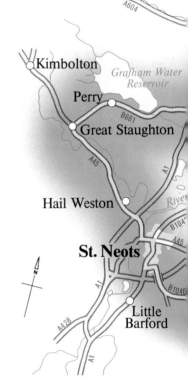

The Old Grammar School Museum at Huntingdon

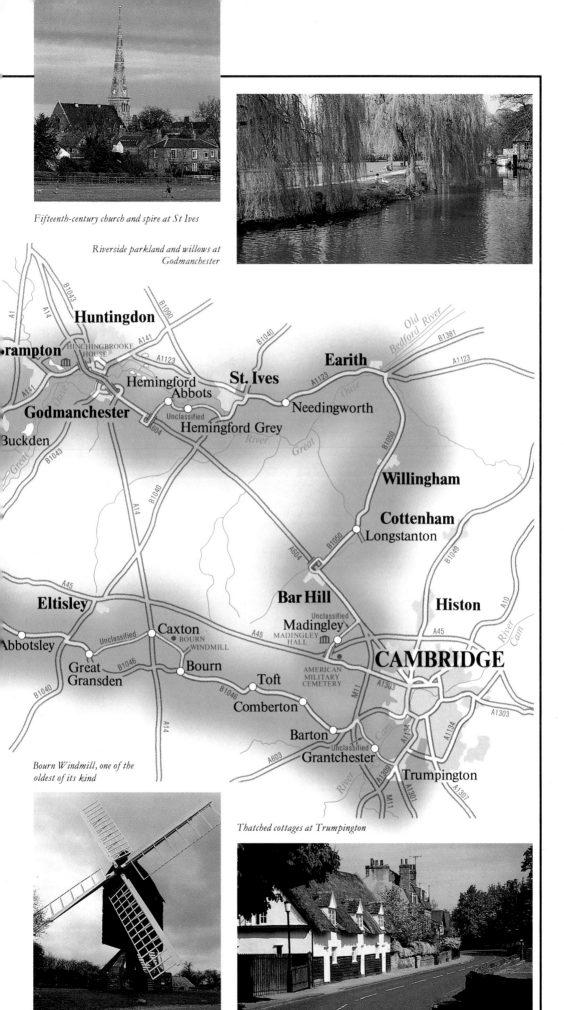

Fifteenth-century church and spire at St Ives

Riverside parkland and willows at Godmanchester

Huntingdon

rampton

HINCHINGBROOKE HOUSE

Hemingford Abbots

St. Ives

Earith

Godmanchester

Unclassified

Needingworth

Buckden

Hemingford Grey

Willingham

Cottenham

Longstanton

Eltisley

Bar Hill

Histon

Caxton

Madingley

BOURN WINDMILL

MADINGLEY HALL

Abbotsley

Unclassified

CAMBRIDGE

Great Gransden

Bourn

AMERICAN MILITARY CEMETERY

Toft

Comberton

Barton

Bourn Windmill, one of the oldest of its kind

Grantchester

Unclassified

Trumpington

Thatched cottages at Trumpington

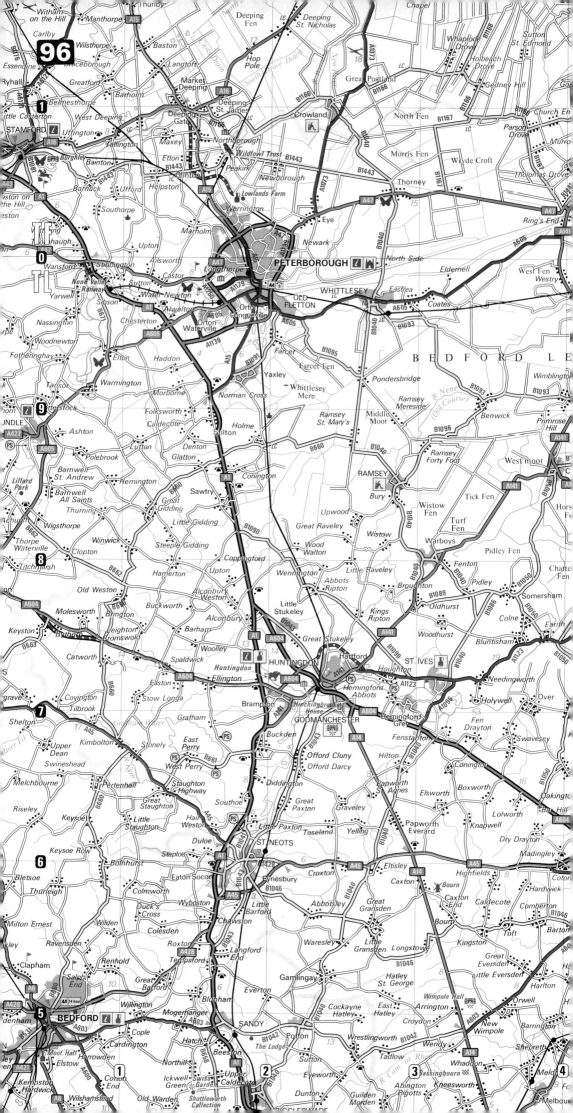

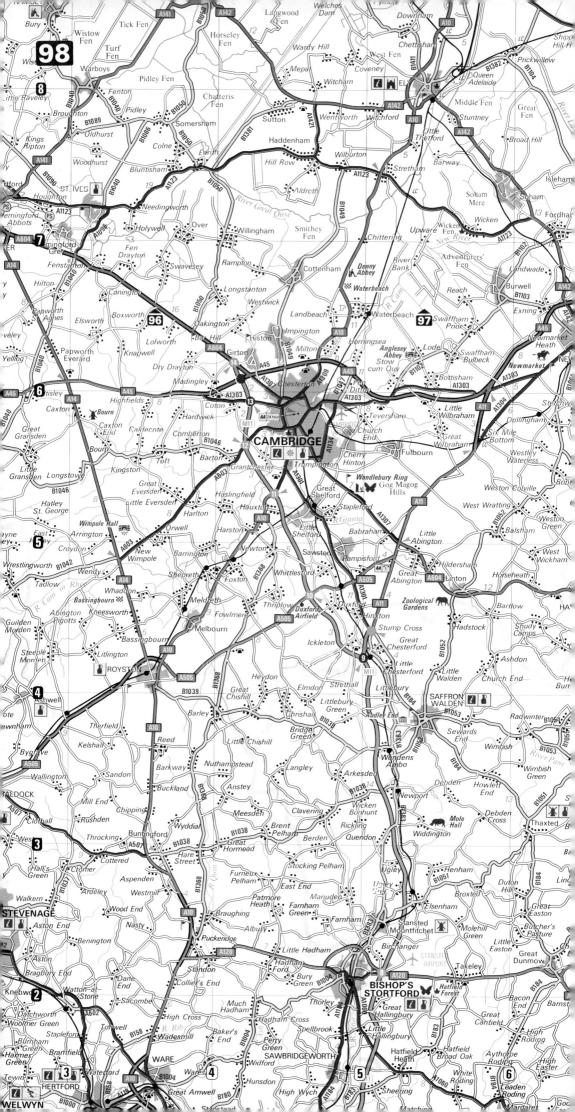

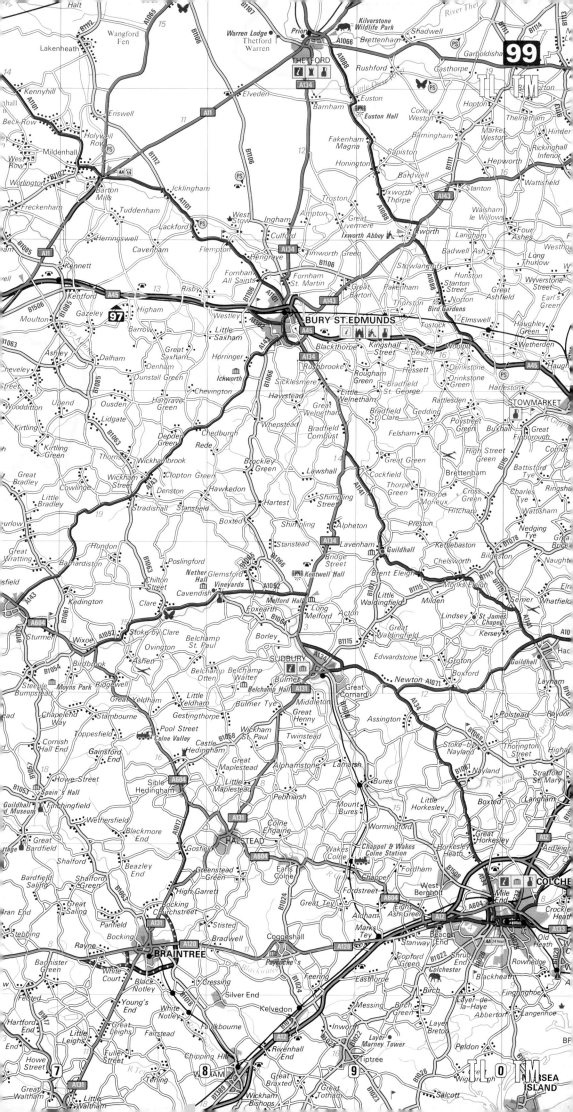

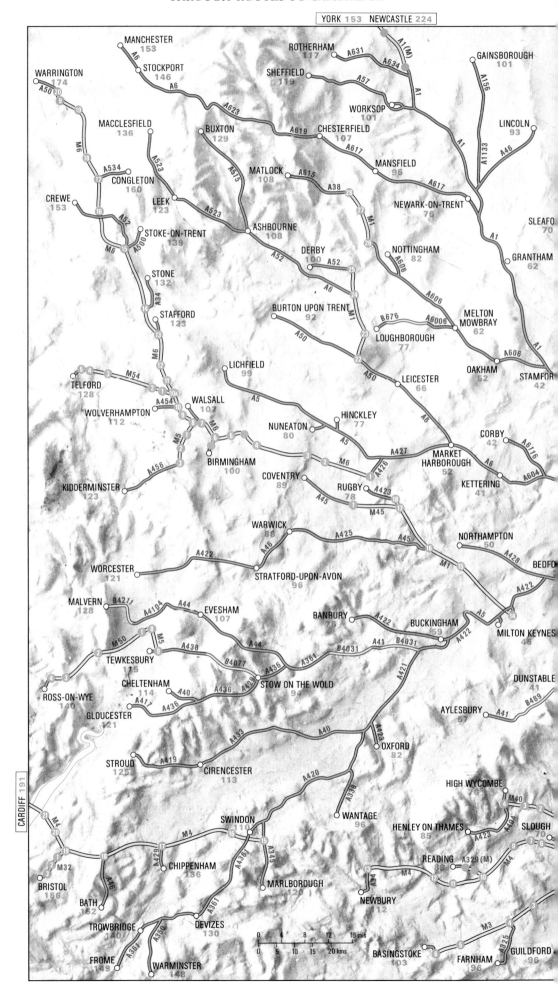

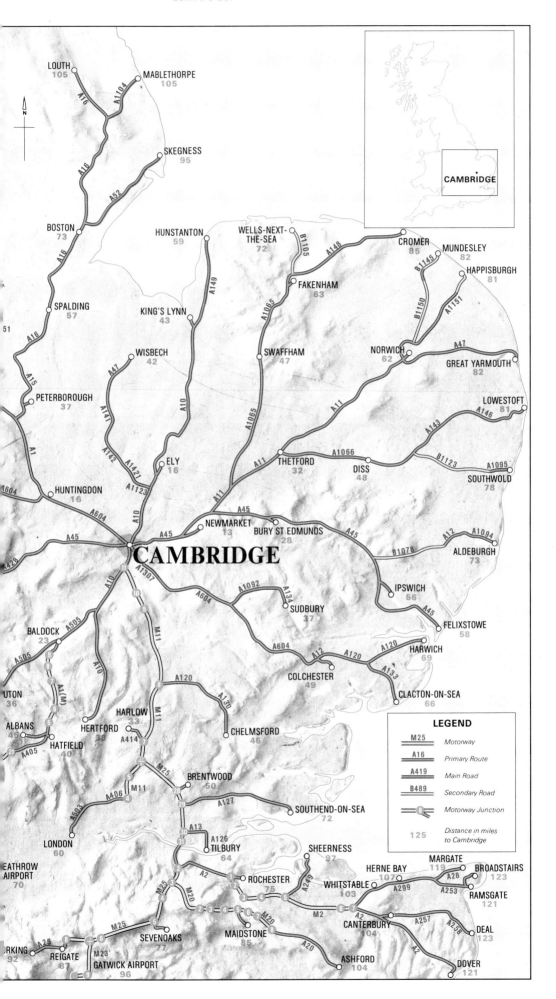

LEGEND

M25	*Motorway*
A16	*Primary Route*
A419	*Main Road*
B489	*Secondary Road*
	Motorway Junction
125	*Distance in miles to Cambridge*

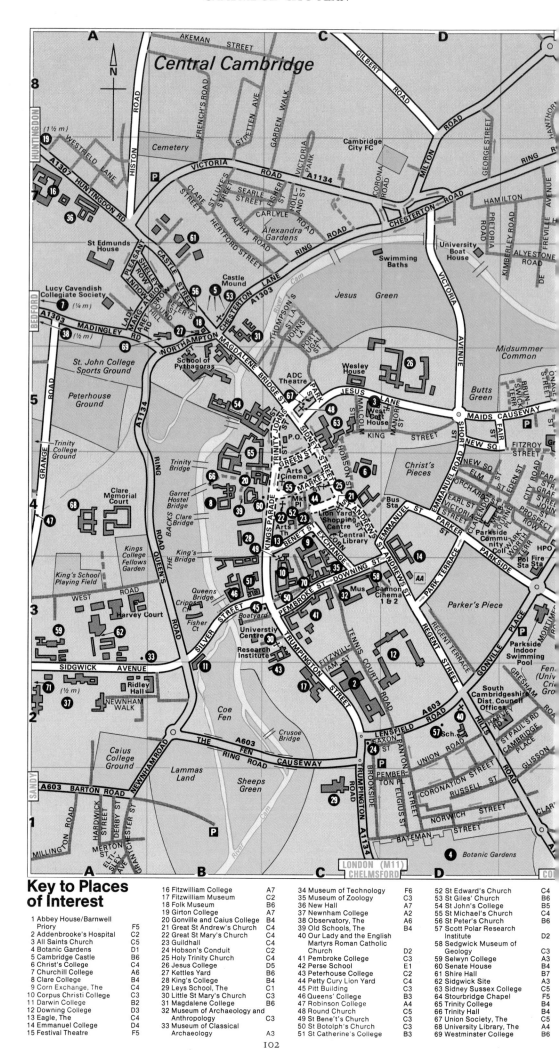

CAMBRIDGE CITY PLAN

Key to Places of Interest

1 Abbey House/Barnwell Priory F5
2 Addenbrooke's Hospital C2
3 All Saints Church C5
4 Botanic Gardens D1
5 Cambridge Castle B6
6 Christ's College C4
7 Churchill College A6
8 Clare College B4
9 Corn Exchange, The C4
10 Corpus Christi College C3
11 Darwin College B2
12 Downing College D3
13 Eagle, The C4
14 Emmanuel College D4
15 Festival Theatre F5

16 Fitzwilliam College A7
17 Fitzwilliam Museum C2
18 Folk Museum B6
19 Girton College A7
20 Gonville and Caius College B4
21 Great St Andrew's Church C4
22 Great St Mary's Church C4
23 Guildhall C4
24 Hobson's Conduit C2
25 Holy Trinity Church C4
26 Jesus College D5
27 Kettles Yard B6
28 King's College B4
29 Leys School, The C1
30 Little St Mary's Church C3
31 Magdalene College B6
32 Museum of Archaeology and Anthropology C3
33 Museum of Classical Archaeology A3

34 Museum of Technology F6
35 Museum of Zoology C3
36 New Hall A7
37 Newnham College A2
38 Observatory, The A6
39 Old Schools, The B4
40 Our Lady and the English Martyrs Roman Catholic Church D2
41 Pembroke College C3
42 Perse School E1
43 Peterhouse College C2
44 Petty Cury Lion Yard C4
45 Pitt Building C3
46 Queens' College B3
47 Robinson College A4
48 Round Church C5
49 St Bene't's Church C3
50 St Botolph's Church C3
51 St Catherine's College B3

52 St Edward's Church C4
53 St Giles' Church B6
54 St John's College B5
55 St Michael's Church C4
56 St Peter's Church B6
57 Scott Polar Research Institute D2
58 Sedgwick Museum of Geology C3
59 Selwyn College A3
60 Senate House B4
61 Shire Hall B7
62 Sidgwick Site A3
63 Sidney Sussex College C5
64 Stourbridge Chapel F5
65 Trinity College B4
66 Trinity Hall B4
67 Union Society, The C5
68 University Library, The A4
69 Westminster College B6

102

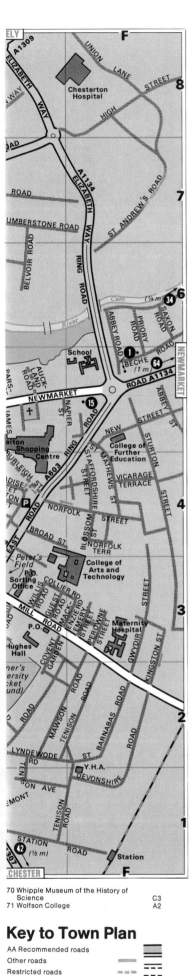

Street Index and Grid Reference

Central Cambridge

Abbey Road	F5-F6
Abbey Street	F5
Akemen Street	A8-B8
Albion Row	A6-B6
Alpha Road	B7-C7-C6
Auckland Road	E5
Aylestone Road	D6-E6
Barton Road	A1
Bateman Street	C1-D1-E1
Beche Road	F5-F6
Belvoir Road	E6-E7
Blossom Street	F4
Broad Street	E4
Brookside Street	C1-C2
Brunswick Terrace	E5
Burleigh Street	E4
Cambridge Place	E2
Carlyle Road	B7-C7
Castle Street	A7-A6-B7-B6
Chesterton Hall Crescent	D7-D8
Chesterton Lane	B6-C6-C7
Chesterton Road	D7-E7-E8
City Road	E4
Claremont	E1
Clarendon Street	D4-E4
Clare Street	B7
Collier Road	E3-F3
Coronation Street	D1-D2
Corn Exchange Street	C3-C4
Covent Garden	E2-E3
De Freville Avenue	E6-E7
Derby Street	A1
Devonshire Road	F1-F2
Downing Street	C3-C4-D3-D4
Earl Street	D4
East Road	E3-E4-F4-F5
Eden Street	E4
Eligius Street	D1
Elizabeth Way	F5-F6-F7-E7-E8
Elm Street	D4-E4
Eltisley Avenue	A1
Emery Street	F3
Emmanuel Road	D4-D5
Emmanuel Street	C4-D4
Fair Street	D5-E5
Fisher Street	C7
Fitzroy Street	E5
Fitzwilliam Street	C2-C3
French's Road	B7-B8
Garden Walk	C7-C8
Gilbert Road	C8-D8
Glisson Road	E1-E2-E3
Gonville Place	D2-D3-E3
Grafton Street	E4
Grange Road	A3-A4-A5-A6
Grantchester Street	A1
Green Street	C4-C5
Gresham Road	E2
Guest Road	E3
Gwydir Street	F2-F3-F4
Hamilton Road	D7-E7-F7
Hardwick Street	A1
Harvey Road	D2-E2
Hertford Street	B7-B6-C6
High Street	E8-F8
Hills Road	D2-E2-E1
Histon Rod	A7-A8-B8
Hobson Street	C4-C5
Holland Street	C7
Humberstone Road	E7-F7
Huntingdon Road	A7
James Street	E5
Jesus Lane	C5-D5
John Street	E4
Kimberley Road	E6-E7
King's Parade	C4-C3
King Street	C4-C5-D5
Kingston Street	F2-F3

Lady Margaret Road	A6
Lensfield Road	C2-D2
Lyndewode Road	E2-F2
Mackenzie Road	E3-F3
Maddingley Road	A6-B6-B5
Magdalene Bridge Street	B6-B5-C5
Malcolm Street	C5
Manor Street	D5
Maids Causeway	D5-E5
Market Street	C4
Mawson Road	E2-F2-F3
Melbourne Place	D4-E4
Merton Street	A1
Millington Road	A1
Milton Road	D7-D8-E8
Mortimer Road	E3
Mount Pleasant	A6-A7
Napier Street	E5
Newmarket Road	E5-F5
Newnham Road	A1-A2-B1-B2
New Square	D4
New Square	D5
New Street	F5
Norfolk Street	E4-F4
Norfolk Terrace	F4
Northampton Street	B5-B6
Norwich Street	D1-E1
Orchard Street	D4-E4
Panton Street	D1-D2
Paradise Street	E4
Parker Street	D4
Parkside Mill Road	D4-D3-E4-E3-F3-F2
Park Street	C5
Park Terrace	D3-D4
Parsonage Street	E5
Pemberton Place	C1-D1
Pembroke Street	C3
Perowne Street	F3
Portugal Street	C6
Pound Hill	B6
Pretoria Road	D6-D7
Prospect Row	E4
Queens Road	B5-A5-A4-B4-B3
Regent Street	D2-D3
Russell Street	D1-E1
Saxon Road	F6
Searle Street	B7-C7
Shelley Row	A6-B6
Short Street	D5
Sidgwick Avenue	A2-B2-B3
Sidney Street	C4-C5
Silver Street	B3-C3
Staffordshire Street	F4
St Andrew's Road	F6-F7-F8
St Andrew's Street	C4-D4-D3
Station Road	E1-F1
St Barnabas Road	F2
St John's Lane	C6
St John's Street	C5
St Luke's Street	B7
St Paul's Road	D2-E2
St Peter's Street	B6
Stretton Avenue	B7-B8-C8
Sturton Street	F3-F4-F5
Tennis Court Road	C3-C2-D2
Tenison Avenue	E1-E2
Tenison Road	E1-F1-F2
The Fen Causeway	B2-C2
Thompson's Lane	C6
Trinity Street	C4-C5
Trumpington Road	C1-C2
Trumpington Street	C2-C3
Union Road	D1-D2
Union Lane	F8
Vicarage Terrace	F4
Victoria Avenue	D5-D6-D7
Victoria Road	A7-B7-C7-D7
Victoria Street	D4
Warkworth Terrace	E3-E4
Westfield Lane	A7-A8
Willis Road	E3

70 Whipple Museum of the History of Science   C3
71 Wolfson College   A2

Key to Town Plan

AA Recommended roads	
Other roads	
Restricted roads	
Buildings of interest	
Churches	†
Car parks	P
Parks and open spaces	
AA Service Centre	AA

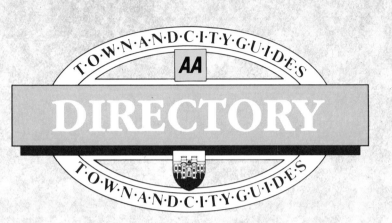

TOWN·AND·CITY·GUIDES

AA

DIRECTORY

TOWN·AND·CITY·GUIDES

The wealth of antiquarian booksellers, galleries and traditional shops of all kinds which tempt the visitor to browse is another of the city's delights

Using the Directory

TELEPHONE NUMBERS

Phone numbers are on the Cambridge exchange (STD code 0223) if no other exchange name or number is given. If just an exchange number is given the exchange name is the same as the entry name.

AA CLASSIFICATIONS
Hotels

★   Good hotels and inns, generally of small scale and with good furnishings and facilities.

★★   Hotels with a higher standard of accommodation. There should be 20% private bathrooms or showers.

★★★   Well-appointed hotels. Two-thirds of the bedrooms should have private bathrooms or showers.

★★★★ Exceptionally well-appointed hotels offering high standards of comfort and service. All bedrooms should have private bathrooms or showers.

★★★★★ Luxury hotels offering the highest international standards.

Restaurants

✕   Modest but good restaurant.

✕✕   Restaurant offering a higher standard of comfort than above.

✕✕✕   Well-appointed restaurant.

✕✕✕✕   Exceptionally well-appointed restaurant.

✕✕✕✕✕ Luxury restaurant.

Camp sites

►   Site licence; 10% of pitches for touring units; site density not more than 30 per acre; 2 separate toilets for each sex per 30 pitches; good quality tapwater; efficient waste disposal; regular cleaning of ablutions block; fire precautions; well-drained ground.

►►   All one-pennant facilities plus: 2 washbasins with hot and cold water for each sex per 30 pitches in separate washrooms; warden available at certain times of the day.

►►►   All two-pennant facilities plus: one shower or bath for each sex per 30 pitches, with hot and cold water; electric shaver points and mirrors; all-night lighting of toilet blocks; deep sinks for washing clothes; facilities for buying milk, bread and gas; warden in attendance by day, on call by night.

►►►►   All three-pennant facilities plus: a higher degree of organisation than one–three pennant sites; attention to landscaping; reception office; late-arrivals enclosure; first-aid hut; shop; routes to essential facilities lit after dark; play area; bad-weather shelter; hard standing for touring vans.

►►►►► A comprehensive range of services and equipment; careful landscaping; automatic laundry; public telephone; indoor play facilities for children; extra facilities for recreation; warden in attendance 24 hours per day.

EGON RONAY

Egon Ronay appointed establishments are indicated by (ER).

AA AND ER GUIDES

For more details on the accommodation and eating out establishments listed, please see the current edition of the AA guides: *Hotels and Restaurants in Britain; Guesthouses, Farmhouses and Inns in Britain; Holiday Homes, Cottages and Apartments in Britain* and *Camping and Caravanning in Britain*, and the Egon Ronay guides: *Healthy Eating Out; Pub Guide; Just a Bite* and *Egon Ronay's Guide to Hotels, Restaurants and Inns*.

ABBREVIATIONS

approx—approximately
appt—appointment
BH—Bank Holiday(s)
Chr—Christmas
EH—English Heritage—buildings in the care of the Historic Buildings and Monuments Commission (used to be known as Ancient Monuments (AM))
ER—Egon Ronay (see above)
Etr—Easter
eve—evening
ex—excluding/except
ext—extension
gps—groups
hr—hour(s)
incl—including/inclusive
m—mile(s)
nr—near
NT—National Trust—Regional Office, Blickling, Norwich *Tel* Aylsham *(0263) 733471/734077*
Tel—telephone
TIC—Tourist Information Centre—addresses and phone numbers in Useful Information section
wk—week(s)
wknd—weekend(s)

The information in this Directory is liable to change at short notice. While every effort has been made to ensure that it is comprehensive and up to date, the publishers cannot accept responsibility for errors or omissions, or for changes in the details given.

Accommodation

Visitors to Cambridge should remember that accommodation is likely to be difficult to find during 'May Week', the Degree Ceremony and the Cambridge Festival. They should book well ahead, particularly at these times.

HOTELS — The AA's choice

★★★★**Garden House,** Granta Place, off Mill Lane (Best Western) *Tel 63421 Telex no 81463*

★★★★**Post House,** Lakeview, Bridge Road, Impington (2½m N, on N side roundabout junction A45/B1049) (Trusthouse Forte) *Tel Histon (022 023) 7000 Telex no 817123*

★★★**University Arms,** Regent Street (Inter Hotel) *Tel 351241 Telex no 817311*

★★★**Cambridgeshire Moat House** (Queens Moat) Bar Hill *Tel Crafts Hill (0954) 80555 Telex no 817141*

★★**Gonville,** Gonville Place *Tel 66611*

★★**Arundel House,** 53 Chesterton Road *Tel 67701 Telex no 817936*

★**Quy Mill,** Newmarket Road, Stow-cum-Quy *Tel Teversham (022 05) 4114*

GUESTHOUSES

Antwerp, 36 Brookfields *Tel 247690*
Ayeone Cleave, 95 Gilbert Road *Tel 63387*
Belle Vue, 33 Chesterton Road *Tel 351859*
Fairways, 143 Cherry Hinton Road *Tel 246063*
Hamilton Hotel, 156 Chesterton Road *Tel 65664*
Helen's Hotel, 167–169 Hills Road *Tel 246465*
Lensfield Hotel, 53 Lensfield Road *Tel 355017*
Sorrento Hotel, 196 Cherry Hinton Road *Tel 243533*
Suffolk House Private Hotel, 69 Milton Road *Tel 352016*

SELF CATERING

20 **Water Street** (*house*), Old Chesterton. *For bookings* Mrs S J Mackay, 'Roebuck House', 28 Ferry Lane, Chesterton, Cambridge *Tel 60000*
Whitehouse Holiday Apartments (*flats*), Conduit Head Road *Tel 67110 & Madingley (0954) 211361* (1¼m from centre of Cambridge, just off the A1303)

CAMP SITES

▶▶▶**Highfield Farm Camping Site,** Long Road, Comberton *Tel (022 026) 2308* (3m W of Cambridge between A45 and A603. From M11 leave junction 12, take A603 ½m then B1046 to Comberton)

Eating & Drinking Out

Angeline (ER), 8 Market Passage *Tel 60305* Closed Sun eve, BH & 3 wk Etr
Charlie Chan (ER), 14 Regent Street *Tel 61763* Closed 25 & 26 Dec. Chinese cooking

Nettles (ER), 6 St Edwards Passage, King's Parade Closed Sun & BH. Wholefood vegetarian
✕ **Peking,** 21 Burleigh Street *Tel 354755* Pekinese cooking

Upstairs (ER), 71 Castle Street *Tel 312569* Closed Mon & 25 & 26 Dec
Waffles (ER), 71 Castle Street *Tel 312569* Closed Mon, 2 wks Sep & 1 wk Chr

Places to Visit

ANCIENT MONUMENTS AND BUILDINGS

See also under Open-air attractions for village reconstructions, etc.
Bury St Edmunds—Abbey ruins (EH). Free
Castle Hedingham—Hedingham Castle *Tel Hedingham (0787) 60261.* Open Etr, May–Oct daily, 10–5. Gps at other times by appt
Denny Abbey (EH), Ely Road, Waterbeach (5m NE Cambridge). Open mid Mar–mid Oct, Wed–Sat, 9.30–6.30, Sun 2–6.30; mid Oct–mid Mar, Sat 9.30–4, Sun 2–4
Royston Cave, Melbourn Street. Open Etr–Sep, Sat, Sun & BH Mon, 2–6
Saffron Walden Maze. Open all year. Free
Thetford Priory (EH). Open all year. Free
Thorney Abbey Church (7m NE Peterborough). Open all year. Free
Weeting—Grimes Graves (EH)

(2m N Brandon) *Tel Thetford (0842) 810656.* Open mid Mar–mid Oct, Mon–Sat 9.30–6.30, Sun 2–6.30; mid Oct–mid Mar, Mon–Sat 9.30–4, Sun 2–4
Widdington (4m S Saffron Walden)—Priors Hall Barn (EH). Open late Mar–late Sep, Sat, Sun & BH, 9.30–6.30

ART GALLERIES IN CAMBRIDGE

Cambridge Holographics, 29 Magdalene Street *Tel 470349.* Open Mon–Sat 10–6, Sun 10.30–6
Fitzwilliam Museum, Trumpington Street *Tel 332900.* Upper galleries (paintings) open Tue–Sat 2–5, Sun 2.15–5. Also Etr, Spring & Aug BH Mons. Closed Good Fri & 24 Dec–1 Jan (incl). Free
Kettle's Yard, Northampton Street/Castle Street *Tel 352124.* Permanent Collection and house open daily 2–4. Exhibition gallery open Tue–Sat 12.30–

5.30 (7pm Thu), Sun 2–5.30. Closed BH & Chr–New Year incl. Gps of 10 or more admitted to Permanent Collection by appt only. Free

ART GALLERIES OUTSIDE CAMBRIDGE

Many of the region's historic houses (see under that heading) also have fine art collections, as do some of the museums such as Lavenham Little Hall.
Bedford—Cecil Higgins Art Gallery & Museum, Castle Close *Tel (0234) 211222.* Open Tue–Fri & BH Mon 12.30–5, Sat 11–5, Sun 2–5. Closed Good Fri & Chr. Free
Bury St Edmunds Art Gallery. Open Tue–Sat 10.30–4.30. Sun by prior arrangement
Peterborough—City Museum & Art Gallery, Priestgate *Tel (0733) 43329,* Open Oct–Apr, Tue–Sat 12–5; May–Sep, Tue–Sat 10–5. Closed Good Fri & Chr. Free
Sudbury—Gainsborough Museum (see under Museums)

CHURCHES AND CATHEDRALS IN CAMBRIDGE

Fuller details, including the locations, of the Cambridge churches listed below are given in the Cambridge – Places to Visit section (see page 34).

All Saints Church (disused)
Great St Mary's Church. Small admission charge for tower
Holy Trinity Church
Little St Mary's Church
Our Lady and the English Martyrs Roman Catholic Church
Round Church
St Andrew the Great Church (disused and only visible from outside)
St Bene't's Church
St Botolph Church
St Edward's Church
St Giles' Church—now houses Brass Rubbing Centre (see Crafts entry in Shopping section)
St Michael's Church
St Peter's Church
Stourbridge Chapel—Key available (see chapel notice board)

CATHEDRALS OUTSIDE CAMBRIDGE

Ely Cathedral
Open winter 7.30 – 6.30, summer 7 – 7. (Admission charge)
Peterborough Cathedral

COLLEGES AND UNIVERSITY BUILDINGS

Fuller details, including the locations, of the Cambridge colleges listed below are given in the city gazetteer section (see page 34); however, the century of foundation of the college—not always the date of the oldest buildings—is given here as a rough guide. In general the colleges are open to visitors between 9am and 5.30pm, but it should be remembered that they are private property and the public have no automatic rights to visit them. The libraries, dining halls and gardens tend to have much more restricted (if any) opening hours, and only those open to the public on a regular basis are included here. The colleges are closed to the public during exam time—May – mid June. Parties of 10 or more people wishing to visit the colleges must be accompanied by a Blue Badged Cambridge Guide—contact the TIC for details.

Christ's College (15C)
Churchill College (20C)
Clare College (14C). Fellows' Garden open Mon – Fri, 2 – 4.45
Corpus Christi College (14C)
Darwin College (20C)
Downing College (19C)
Emmanuel College (16C)
Fitzwilliam College (20C)
Girton College (19C)

Gonville and Caius College (14C)
Jesus College (15C). Chapel open 6am – 10pm
King's College (15C). Chapel normally open term-time Mon – Sat 9 – 3.45 & Sun 2 – 3, 4.30 – 5.45; vacations Mon – Sat 9 – 5, Sun 10.30 – 5. Choral services term-time 5.30 (Tue – Sat) & 10.30 & 3.30 (Sun)
Magdalene College (16C). Pepys Library open Mon – Sat 2.30 – 3.30 (Oct – Dec & Jan – Mar term-times), 11.30 – 12.30 & 2.30 – 3.30 (Apr (term-time)— late Aug)
New Hall (20C)
Newnham College (19C)
Pembroke College (14C)
Peterhouse (13C)
Queens' College (15C). Open 1.45 – 4.30 (small admission charge)
Robinson College (20C)
St Catharine's College (15C)
St John's College (16C). Chapel normally open term-time Tue – Fri 9 – 12 & 2 – 4, Sat & Mon 9 – 12. Services during term-time Tue – Sat 6.30, Sun 10.30 & 6.30
Selwyn College (19C)
Sidney Sussex College (16C)
Trinity College (16C). Wren Library open Mon – Fri 12 – 2 & Sat (term-time only) 10.30 – 12.30, closed BH. Chapel services during term-time Sun 6.15 & Wed 6.30
Trinity Hall (14C)
University Library—guided tours 3pm Mon – Fri
Westminster College (19C)
Wolfson College (20C)

GARDENS IN CAMBRIDGE

Botanic Garden. Entrances on Hills Road, Bateman Street and Trumpington Road.
Open Mon – Sat 8 – 6.30 (or dusk if earlier), Sun May – Sep 2.30 – 6.30 (or dusk). Glasshouses open 11 – 12.30 & 2 – 4. Free
Clare College—Fellows' Garden (see under Colleges)

GARDENS OUTSIDE CAMBRIDGE

Many of the historic houses in the area have fine gardens. Unless stated otherwise the gardens are open at the same time as the house.
Buckden Palace.
Gardens open May – Aug 10 – 6, Sep – Apr 10 – 4. Interior open Jun – Aug, Tue, 2.30 – 5. Free
Finchingfield—Spains Hall. Open May – Jul Sun & May BH 2 – 5
Saffron Walden—Bridge End Gardens *Tel Great Dunmow (0371) 5411*.
Open all year daily 9 – dusk. Free

HISTORIC HOUSES AND CASTLES

Anglesey Abbey (NT), Lode (6m NE Cambridge) *Tel 811200*.
House open mid Apr – mid Oct,

Wed – Sun & BH, 1.30 – 5.30. Gardens open Apr – June Wed – Sun, late Jun – Oct daily, 1.30 – 5.30. Times may vary slightly from year to year. Separate entrance fee for gardens only available. (See also Lode Watermill under Open-air attractions)
Audley End House (EH) (nr Saffron Walden) *Tel Saffron Walden (0799) 22399*.
House open Etr – Sep, Tue – Sun 1 – 5, grounds 12 – 6.30 (& also most of Oct). Also BH Mon
Buckden Palace (see under Gardens outside Cambridge)
Burghley House (1m SE Stamford) *Tel Stamford (0780) 52451*.
Open Etr – Oct daily 11 – 5, Good Fri 2 – 5. Usually closed for one day in early Sep
Euston Hall (3m S Thetford) *Tel Thetford (0842) 66366*.
Open early Jun – late Sep, Thu 2.30 – 5.30
Godmanchester—Island Hall, Post Street *Tel Huntingdon (0480) 59676*.
Open Jun – mid Sep, Sun 2.30 – 5.30. Gps by appt at other times
Halstead—Gosfield Hall. Open May – Sep Wed & Thu 2 – 5 with guided tours (obligatory) at 2.30 & 3.15
Hinchingbrooke House (1½m W Huntingdon) *Tel Huntingdon (0480) 51121*.
Open Apr – Aug, Sun & BH Mon 1 – 5. Gps by appt at other times
Ickworth (NT), Horringer (3m SW Bury St Edmunds). *Tel Horringer (028 488) 270*.
Open May – Sep daily (ex Mon & Thu) & BH Mon 1.30 – 5.30. Apr & Oct wknd only. Park open daily dawn to dusk
Kimbolton Castle (7m NW St Neots) *Tel Huntingdon (0480) 860505*.
Open Etr, Spring BH wknd & mid Jul – Aug Sun 2 – 6
Lavenham—The Priory, Water Street *Tel (0787) 247417*.
Open daily (ex Sun) Etr – Oct 10.30 – 12.30 & 2 – 5.30
Long Melford—Kentwell Hall *Tel Sudbury (0787) 310207*.
Open Etr Fri – Tue then Etr – mid Jun, Wed, Thu, Sun 2 – 6; mid Jun – mid Jul, Sat & Sun only 11 – 5 (historical re-creations); mid Jul – Sep, Wed – Sun 2 – 6. Admission fee for gardens and animals only available
Long Melford—Melford Hall (NT).
Open early Apr – late Sep, Wed, Thu, Sun & BH Mon, & Sat Jun – Aug 2 – 6.
Longthorpe Tower (EH) (2m W Peterborough).
Open mid Mar – mid Oct, Tue & Sun 2 – 6.30, Wed – Sat 9.30 – 6.30; mid Oct – mid Mar as summer but closes at 4pm

Oxborough—Oxburgh Hall (NT) (7m SW Swaffham). *Tel Gooderstone (036 621) 258.* Open May–Sep daily (ex Thu & Fri) 1.30–5.30, BH Mon 11–5.30. Also late Apr & early Oct Sat & Sun 1.30–5.30

Wimpole Hall (NT) (8m SW Cambridge) *Tel 207257.* Open mid Apr–late Oct daily (ex Mon & Fri), 1–5 & BH Mon. Home Farm open from 11

Wisbech—Peckover House (NT), North Brink *Tel (0945) 583463.* Open May–Sep, Sat–Wed & also late Apr & early Oct Sat, Sun & BH Mon, 2–5.30. Gps by appt

MILITARY CEMETERY

Madingley (4m W Cambridge)—American Military Cemetery *Tel (0954) 210350.* Open May–Sep 8–6, Oct–Apr, 9–dusk

MUSEUMS IN CAMBRIDGE

Many of the museums listed here are attached to University departments. Their opening hours tend to be limited so check times carefully to avoid a wasted journey.

Fitzwilliam Museum, Trumpington Street *Tel 332900.* Open Tue–Sat (Lower galleries 10–2, Upper galleries 2–5); Sun (all galleries) 2.15–5. Also Etr, Spring & Aug BH Mons. Closed Good Fri & 24 Dec–1 Jan (incl). Free

Folk Museum, Castle Street *Tel 355159.* Open Tue–Sat 10.30–5, Sun 2.30–4.30 (closed BH). Opening times subject to revision

Museum of Archaeology and Anthropology, Downing Street *Tel 333510.* Open Mon–Fri 2–4, Sat 10–12.30. Closed Etr wk, 24 Dec–1 Jan (incl) & some BH. Free

Museum of Classical Archaeology, Sidgwick Avenue *Tel 335153.* Open Mon–Fri 9–1, 2.15–5; Sat (term-time only) 9–1. Closed Chr & Etr. Free

Museum of Technology, Riverside (off Newmarket Road) *Tel 68650.* Open first Sun in every month, 2–6 (static). Pumping engine in steam approx 5 wknd during year, dates from TIC

Museum of Zoology, Downing Street *Tel 336600.* Open Mon–Fri 2.15–4.45. Closed Etr, Chr & BH. Student gps at other times by appt. Free

Scott Polar Research Institute, Lensfield Road *Tel 336540.* Open all year Mon–Sat 2.30–4. Closed some BH. Free

Sedgwick Museum of Geology, Downing Street *Tel 333400.* Open all year Mon–Fri 9–1, 2–5; Sat (term-time only) 10–1. Closed Chr & some BH

Whipple Museum of the History of Science, Free School Lane *Tel 334540.* Open Mon–Fri 2–4 (closed BH & university vacations). Also open first Sun in the month all year. Free

MUSEUMS OUTSIDE CAMBRIDGE

Ashwell—Village Museum, Swan Street *Tel (046 274) 2155.* Open Sun & BH 2.30–5. Gps by appt at other times

Bedford Museum, Castle Lane *Tel (0234) 53323.* Open all year Tue–Sat 11–5, Sun 2–5. Closed Mon (ex BH afternoons), Good Fri & Chr. Free

Bedford—Bunyan Museum, Mill Street *Tel (0234) 58870/58627.* Open Apr–Sep, Tue–Sat 2–4

Bedford—Cecil Higgins Art Gallery & Museum (see under Art galleries)

Bedford—Elstow Moot Hall (1½m SW) *Tel (0234) 66889.* Open Apr–Oct, Tue–Sat & BH 2–5, Sun 2–5.30

Bishop's Stortford—Rhodes Memorial Museum and Commonwealth Centre, South Road *Tel (0279) 51746.* Open Mon & Wed–Sat 10–4, Tue 10–12. Closed early Aug, Sun & BH

Bury St Edmunds—Gershom-Parkington Collection of Clocks Watches, Angel Corner, Angel Hill *Tel (0284) 63233 ext 227.* Open Mon–Sat 10–5, Sun 2–5. Closed Chr, New Year & Good Fri. Free

Bury St Edmunds—Moyses Hall Museum, Cornhill *Tel (0284) 63233 ext 236.* Open Mar–Oct, Mon–Sat 10–1, 2–5; Nov–Feb, Mon–Sat 10–1, 2–4. Closed winter BH, Good Fri, Etr Sat & May Day BH

Bury St Edmunds—Suffolk Regiment Museum, Gibraltar Barracks, Out Risbygate *Tel (0284) 2394.* Open Mon–Fri 10–12, 2–4. Closed BH and occasionally at other times. Free

Cavendish—Sue Ryder Foundation Museum *Tel Glemsford (0787) 280252.* Open Mon–Sat 10–5.30, Sun 10–11 & 12.15–5.30

Chatteris Museum, Grove House, High Street *Tel (03543) 2414.* Open Thu 2–4 and by appt. Free

Clare—Ancient House Museum, High Street *Tel (0787) 277865.* Open mid Apr–mid Oct, Wed–Sun & BH 2.30–4.30, Sun 11–12.30

Ely Museum, Sacrist's Gate, High Street *Tel (0353) 2516.* Open Oct–May, Sat & Sun 2–4.15; Jun–Sep, Thu, Sat & Sun 2–5. Visits at other times by appt

Ely—Stained Glass Museum, Ely

Cathedral *Tel (0353) 5103.* Open Mar–Oct, Mon–Fri 10.30–4, Sat & BH 10.30–4.30, Sun 12–3

Finchingfield—Guildhall & Museum. Open Etr–Sep, Sun & BH 2.30–6.30. Free

Halstead—Brewery Chapel Museum, Adams Court. Open Apr–Oct, Sat 10–12.30, 2–4.30, Sun 2–4.30. Free

Hinchingbrooke House (see under Historic houses)

Huntingdon—Cromwell Museum, Grammar School Walk *Tel (0480) 425830.* Open Nov–Mar, Tue–Fri 2–5, Sat 11–1, 2–4, Sun 2–4; Apr–Oct, Tue–Fri 11–1, 2–5, Sat & Sun 11–1, 2–4. Closed Chr wk & BH ex Good Fri. Free

King's Lynn—Lynn Museum, Market Street *Tel (0553) 775001.* Open Mon–Sat 10–5. Closed BH, Chr & New Year

King's Lynn—Museum of Social History, 27 King Street *Tel (0553) 775004.* Open Tue–Sat 10–5. Closed BH, Chr & New Year

King's Lynn—Regalia Rooms, Trinity Guildhall. Heritage Centre open Apr–Oct, Mon–Sat 10–4. Other exhibitions open all year 10–4

King's Lynn—St George's Guildhall (NT), King Street. Open Mon–Fri 10.30–5, Sat 10–12.30 (ex when rehearsals in progress). Closed Good Fri, Chr & New Year. Free

Lavenham—Guildhall (NT). Open early Apr–Oct daily 11–1 & 2–5.30

Lavenham—Little Hall, Market Place *Tel (0787) 247179.* Open Etr–mid Oct, Sat, Sun & BH 2.30–6 or by appt

March—March & District Museum, High Street *Tel (0354) 55300.* Open Wed 10–12, Sat 10–12, 2–4. Gps by appt. Free

Mildenhall—Museum, King Street. Open Wed–Sun 2.30–4.30 (Fri 11–4.30). Free

Newmarket—National Horse-Racing Museum, 99 High Street *Tel (0638) 667333.* Open late Mar–early Dec, Tue–Sat, BH Mon & Mon in Aug 10–5, Sun 2–5

Peterborough—City Museum & Art Gallery, Priestgate *Tel (0733) 43329.* Open Oct–Apr, Tue–Sat 12–5; May–Sep, Tue–Sat 10–5. Closed Good Fri & Chr. Free

Royston Museum, Lower King Street *Tel (0763) 42587.* Open Wed & Sat 10–5. Free

Saffron Walden Museum, Museum Street *Tel (0799) 22494.* Open Tue–Sat 10–5 (4pm Oct–Mar), Sun & BH 2.30–5. Closed Good Fri & 24/25 Dec. Free

St Ives—Norris Library & Museum, The Broadway *Tel (0480) 65101*. Open Oct–Apr, Tue–Fri 10–1, 2–4, Sat 10–12; May–Sep, Tue–Fri 10–1, 2–5, Sat 10–12, 2–5. Closed BH wknd. Gps at other times by appt. Free

St Neots—Longsands Museum, Longsands Road *Tel Huntingdon (0480) 72740*. By appt only during school opening hours. Free

Sudbury—Gainsborough Museum, Gainsborough Street *Tel (0787) 72958*. Open Tue–Sat 10–5, Sun & BH Mon 2–5. Closed Good Fri & Chr–New Year, & at 4pm Oct–mid Apr

Thaxted—Guildhall, Town Street. Open Etr–Sep, Sun 2–6; BH wknd, Sat–Mon 11–6, also Good Fri 2–6

Thetford—Ancient House Museum, White Hart Street *Tel (0842) 2599*. Open Mon–Sat 10–5 (closed Mon 1–2); Sun 2–5 (late May–late Sep only). Closed Good Fri, Chr & New Year

Whittlesey—Whittlesea Museum, Market Street *Tel Turves (073 120) 280*. Open Fri & Sun 2.30–4.30, Sat 10–12. Closed BH

Wisbech—Wisbech & Fenland Museum, Museum Square *Tel (0945) 583817*. Open Tue–Sat 10–4 (10–5 Apr–Sep). Closed BH. Free

NATURE RESERVES AND TRAILS

CAMBIENT—contact Cambridge and Isle of Ely Naturalists' Trust, 5 Fulbourn Manor, Manor Walk, Fulbourn *Tel 880788* for details of reserves in Cambridgeshire

Sandy—RSPB reserve. Open daily

Welney Wildfowl Refuge, nr March *Tel Ely (0353) 860711*. Open daily 10–5 (ex Chr). Gp visits for early evening in winter bookable in advance. Also birdwatching hides at Ouse Washes (nr Chatteris) and at Welches Dam

Wicken Fen (NT) *Tel Ely (0353) 720274*. Open daily. Parties by appt only

Nature trails at Clare Castle Country Park, Grafham Water, Hatfield Forest and Wandlebury

OPEN-AIR ATTRACTIONS

See also under Gardens, Nature reserves, Vineyards and Zoos.

Audley End Miniature Railway. Open Apr–Sep, Sat, Sun & BH Mon & daily (ex Mon) during school holidays, 2–6

Cockley Cley—Iceni Village & Museum (3m SW Swaffham) *Tel Swaffham (0760) 21339*. Open Etr–Oct daily 2–5.30; mid Jul–mid Sep daily 11.30–

5.30. Gps by appt

Colne Valley Railway, Castle Hedingham Station (4m NW Halstead) *Tel Hedingham (0787) 61174*. Static displays open daily (ex 24 Dec–Feb) 11–5. Gps by appt in evenings. Steam days Etr–Oct, 1st & 3rd Sun of month & BH Sun & Mon, 12–5

Duxford—Imperial War Museum, Duxford Airfield (8m S Cambridge) *Tel 833963*. Open mid Mar–early Nov daily (ex Good Fri & May Day BH) 10.30–5.30 (last admission 4.45 or dusk). Occasional flying days, dates from TIC or *Tel 835000*

Great Gransden Post Mill (10m W Cambridge off B1046) Open Apr–Oct 9–6. Details of key holders from Post Office.

Haddenham—Farmland Museum, High Street *Tel Ely (0353) 740381*. Open first Sun each month 2–5 & each Wed 10–5 from May–Oct

Houghton Mill (NT) (2m from Huntingdon). Open mid Apr–mid Sep daily (ex Thu & Fri), mid Sep–mid Oct Sat & Sun only, 2–5.30

Lode Watermill (NT). Open mid Apr–mid Oct, wknd & BH Mon 1.30–5.30. Included in Anglesey Abbey admission fee. Corn grinding demonstrations on BH Mon & first Sun of month

Mildenhall Air Show. Contact TIC for details and dates.

Nene Valley Railway Museum, Wansford Station, Stibbington (7m W Peterborough) *Tel Stamford (0780) 782854*. Please phone or contact TIC for details of opening times and train running times

Old Warden (nr Biggleswade)—Shuttleworth Collection of Historic Aeroplanes and Cars *Tel Northill (076 727) 288*. Open daily 10.30–5.30 (last admission 4.30). Closed 1 wk at Chr

Ramsey Rural Museum, The Woodyard *Tel (0487) 813223*. Open Apr–Sep, Sun 2–5. Free

Peterborough—East of England Show at Showground, Alwalton, in July *Tel (0733) 234451*

Sacrewell Mill and Grassyard Collection, Thornhaugh (8m W Peterborough off A47) *Tel Stamford (0780) 782222*. Open late Apr–mid Oct, Sun 2–6. Groups by appt at other times.

Stansted Mountfitchet—Mountfitchet Castle *Tel Bishop's Stortford (0279) 813237*. Open daily mid Mar–mid Nov, 10–5

Stansted Mountfitchet—Windmill *Tel Bishop's Stortford (0279) 812096*. Open 2.30–6.30 Apr–Oct first Sun in month & all Sun in Aug.

Also Etr, May, Spring & Aug BH Sun & Mon. Other times by prior appt

Stowmarket—Museum of East Anglian Life *Tel (0449) 612229*. Open late Mar–late Oct, Mon–Sat 11–5, Sun 12–5 (Jun–Aug 12–6)

Stretham Beam Engine, nr Ely. Open daily 9–6

Thaxted—John Webb's Windmill *Tel (0371) 830366*. Open May–Sep, Sat, Sun & BH, 2–6

West Stow Anglo-Saxon Village (7m NW Bury St Edmunds) *Tel Culford (028 484) 718*. Open Apr–Oct, Tue–Sat 2–5, Sun & BH 11–1 & 2–5. Surrounding parkland open 9–1hr before sunset. Gps by prior appt

Wimpole Hall (NT)—Home Farm. Open mid Apr–late Oct, 11–5 daily (ex Mon & Fri)

VINEYARDS

Cavendish—Nether Hall Manor *Tel Glemsford (0787) 280221*. Open all year daily, 11–4

Felsted Vineyards, Cricks Green *Tel Chelmsford (0245) 361504*. Open all year by appt, but casual visitors also welcome

Linton—Chilford Hundred Vineyard, Balsham Road *Tel 892641*. Open May–Sep, Tue–Sat 10–5, Sun 11–5. Gps by appt at other times

ZOOS AND ANIMAL COLLECTIONS

See also farm museums listed under Open-air attractions.

Kilverstone Wildlife Park (1m E Thetford) *Tel Thetford (0842) 3369*. Open daily 10–6.30 (or dusk in winter)

Linton Zoo, Hadstock Road *Tel 891308*. Open daily (ex 25 Dec) 10–7 (or dusk). Last admission ½hr before closing

Long Melford—Kentwell Hall (rare breeds) see under Historic houses

Norton Tropical Bird Gardens (7m E Bury St Edmunds) *Tel Pakenham (0359) 30957*. Open all year daily 11–6 or dusk

Peakirk (Wildfowl Trust) (5m N Peterborough) *Tel Peterborough (0733) 252271*. Open daily (ex 24 & 25 Dec), 9.30–5.30 (or dusk Nov–Mar); also Sep–Apr first Mon in month to 7.30pm

Shepreth—Willers Mill Fish Farm and Animal Sanctuary, Station Road *Tel Royston (0763) 61832*. Open Mar–Nov, 10.30–6.30 (or dusk)

Widdington (nr Newport)—Mole Hall Wildlife Park *Tel Saffron Walden (0799) 40400*. Open mid Mar–early Nov 10.30–6 daily

Entertainment

Besides the entertainments listed below there are concerts, theatre, films, dances, etc. at festivals and special events both within and outside Cambridge. The local Tourist Information Centres (see Useful Information section) or in Cambridge the City Amenities and Recreation Department (*Tel 358977*) can supply full details, but the main events are listed below.

Bury St Edmunds Festival (May)
Bury St Edmunds—various music recitals, films, concerts, etc. at the Art Gallery *Tel (0284) 62081*
Cambridge—'May Week' events (early Jun)
Cambridge Festival and Cambridge Folk Festival (late Jul). Details available May onwards *Tel 358977*
King's Lynn Festival (late Jul–Aug, based at Fermoy Centre)
Long Melford—Kentwell Hall (historic re-creations mid Jun–mid Jul wknds, and other events during year—*Tel Sudbury (0787) 310207*)

Tickets for a variety of local events may be obtained from the Cambridge Box Office at the Corn Exchange, Wheeler Street *Tel 357851*.

BINGO

Coral Social Club, 21 Hobson Street
Tel 356630

CINEMA

Cannon 1 & 2, St Andrew's Street
Tel 64537
Arts Cinema, Market Passage
Tel 352001
Victoria 1 & 2, Market Hill
Tel 352677 (recorded messages—programmes) or *60061* (other enquiries)

DANCING

Cambridge has a number of groups specialising in particular types of dance (e.g. Traditional English Country, Modern and Old Time Sequence, Scottish, Morris, Country) most of whom would welcome visitors to their meetings (details from TIC).
The Cambridge International Club, 4a Downing Place *Tel 352384* organises Mon evening folk dances for student visitors.

Dinner dances:
Cambridgeshire Moat House, Bar Hill, nr Cambridge *Tel Crafts Hill (0954) 80555* (all year)
Garden House Hotel, Granta Place *Tel 63421* (Nov & Dec)
The University Arms Hotel, Regent Street *Tel 351241* (Nov–Apr)
The University Centre, Granta Place *Tel 63365* (Dec)

DISCOS AND LIVE BANDS

Ronelles International, Heidelberg Gardens, Lion Yard *Tel 64222* (disco diner)
Route 66, Wheeler Street *Tel 357503* (disco diner)
Sea Cadet Hall, Riverside (live bands perform most Sat evenings)

MUSIC—CLASSICAL

Cambridge University Music School, West Road *Tel 335176*.
Concerts during term time. Details from Music School, TIC, Public Library.
Cambridge Symphony Orchestra, details of concerts *Tel 65374*
Corn Exchange concerts, see TIC for details or *Tel 357851*

MacKenzie Society concerts at Carpenter Hall, Victoria Street, Tue (during term-time) 7.45pm *Tel Histon (022 023) 2915*

MUSIC IN CAMBRIDGE PUBS

The Alma, Russell Court (off Russell Street) *Tel 64965* (Sat—rhythm & blues)
The Burleigh Arms, Newmarket Road *Tel 316881* (live bands regularly, Sun lunchtime—jazz)
The Cambridge Arms, King Street *Tel 359650* (Mon—various, Tue & Sun—jazz)
The Geldart, 1 Ainsworth Street *Tel 355983* (Tue & Sun—folk)
The Man on the Moon, Norfolk Street *Tel 350610* (Mon—traditional jazz, Wed—mainstream, Fri—modern jazz, Sat—country & western)
The Salisbury Arms, Tenison Road *Tel 60363* (occasional Sun lunchtime—jazz)

NIGHT CLUBS

Newmarket—The Cabaret Club, 146 High Street *Tel (0638) 668601*

THEATRES IN CAMBRIDGE

ADC Theatre, Park Street *Tel 352001* (Box Office) or *359547* (general)
Arts Theatre, Peas Hill *Tel 352000* (Box Office) or *355246* (general)
Mumford Theatre (CCAT), East Road *Tel 352932*

THEATRES OUTSIDE CAMBRIDGE

Bury St Edmunds—Theatre Royal *Tel (0284) 5127*
King's Lynn—Fermoy Centre *Tel (0553) 774725*
Peterborough—Key Theatre *Tel (0733) 52437*
Sudbury—Quay Theatre *Tel (0787) 74745*
Wisbech—Angles Theatre *Tel (0945) 63607*

Sports and Recreation

GENERAL

Details are given below of the main venues for spectator sports, as well as facilities available for public use in Cambridge. Where certain sports facilities are not available in the city, those in other nearby towns are mentioned. The Eastern Council for Sport and Recreation, 26 Bromham Road, Bedford *Tel (0234) 45222* can supply further information about the availability of sports facilities and coaching courses, as can the City Amenities and Recreation Department

(*Tel 358977*) in Cambridge itself.
Use of tennis courts and bowling greens can usually be arranged on the spot, but other pitches will need to be booked with the Cambridge Sports Pitch Booking Clerk *Tel 248229* (afternoons only).
Local clubs and societies for various sports and recreational hobbies will often welcome visitors. Details are available from the TIC and Public Library.

MULTI-SPORT FACILITIES

Kelsey Kerridge Sports Hall, Gonville Place *Tel 68791*.

Large and small halls, squash courts, projectile gallery, etc. Bar & café.
Day membership available, but advance booking advisable.
Sporturf Pitch, Abbey Sports Centre, Coldham's Common. Artificial grass pitch with floodlighting, changing rooms, showers, etc.
Suitable for soccer and hockey, also five-a-side football, netball, cricket and tennis.
Advance booking with Cambridge Sports Pitch Booking Clerk *Tel 248229* (afternoons).

Huntingdon Recreation Centre, St Peter's Road Tel (0480) 54130. Swimming pool and two squash courts

Peterborough—Ferry Meadows, Nene Valley Park. Water-sports and other facilities Tel (0733) 234443

St Ives—St Ivo Recreation Centre, Westwood Road Tel (0480) 64601. Sports hall, projectile hall, squash courts, bowling rinks, solarium

Wisbech—Hudson Sports Centre, Harecroft Road Tel (0945) 584230. Swimming pool, sports hall, bowling rinks

Also Sports Centres at Bury St Edmunds, Ely, Great Dunmow, Mepal, Soham and Thetford

ANGLING

See under Fishing

BOARDSAILING

Peterborough Sailboard Club Tel (0733) 62858

BOAT HIRE

See Transport section

BOWLS

Greens at Alexandra Gardens, Barnwell Recreation Ground, Christ's Pieces, Coleridge Recreation Ground, Jesus Green, Lammas Land, Romsey Recreation Ground, Nightingale Avenue and King George V Recreation Ground.

CRICKET

First-class cricket matches held at Fenner's, the University cricket ground off Gresham Road.

Local club matches on Parker's Piece, and this and King George V Recreation Ground, Trumpington, available to hire.

FISHING

Rod licences for the Cam, the Ouse and tributary waters available from fishing tackle shops or Anglian Water Authority (Cambridge Division), Clarendon Road, Cambridge Tel 61561. Permits also needed for some waters.

More general information on fishing in East Anglia from Anglian Water, Ambury Road, Huntingdon Tel (0480) 56181

FOOTBALL (SOCCER)

Cambridge United (professional soccer club). Ground at Newmarket Road.

Pitches available at Abbey Sports Centre (Coldham's Common), Cherry Hinton Recreation Ground, Jesus Green, Trumpington and Chesterton Recreation Grounds. Junior pitches at Coleridge and Nuns Way Recreation Grounds.

GOLF

Cambridgeshire Moat House Hotel Golf Club, Bar Hill, nr Cambridge Tel Crafts Hill (0954) 80098. (18 hole Championship Course, undulating park with lake)

Girton Golf Club, Dodford Lane, Girton Tel 276169. Non-members Mon–Fri only, advance booking advisable (18 hole, parkland)

Gog Magog Golf Club, Babraham Road, Cambridge Tel 247628. Users must be golf club members or introduced by a member of Gog Magog Club, Mon–Fri only and advance booking essential (18 hole and new 9 hole course)

Also golf clubs at Bury St Edmunds, Downham Market, Ely, Huntingdon, King's Lynn, Newmarket, Peterborough, Saffron Walden, St Neots, Stowmarket, Sudbury, Swaffham and Thetford.

HOCKEY

Pitches on Parker's Piece and Jesus Green

HORSE-RACING

Newmarket—Racing Apr–Oct. For details Tel (0638) 664151

PETANQUE (BOULES)

Abbey Sports Centre, Coldham's Common

POINT TO POINT

Meetings at Cottenham and Brampton. Contact TIC for details

RIDING

Gransden Hall Riding School, Great Gransden (12m W Cambridge) Tel (076 77) 366

Lodge Riding Stables, Great Abington (7m SE Cambridge) Tel 891101

Park House Stables Riding School, Harston (6m SW Cambridge) Tel 870075

Miss Pickard's School, New Farm Stables, Bourn (8m W Cambridge) Tel Caxton (095 44) 501

Sawston Riding School, Common Lane Farm, Sawston (6m S Cambridge) Tel 835198

Mrs Turner, Broadway Farm, Lolworth (6m NW Cambridge) Tel Madingley (0954) 80159. Facilities for the disabled

Windmill Stables, Shepreth Road, Barrington (7m SW Cambridge) Tel 871487

ROWING

University 'Bumps' held in Feb and Jun (May Week), City 'Bumps' in Jul. Course between Bait's Bite Lock, Milton, and Stourbridge Common. At other times of year rowers may be seen practising on the river from Midsummer Common northwards.

'Leisure' rowing boats available for hire—see under Boat hire in Transport section.

RUGBY

University Rugby Union team plays on first-class ground in Grange Road.

SKATING

East of England Ice Rink, Mallard Road, Bretton, nr Peterborough Tel (0733) 260222

Rollerbury, Station Hill, Bury St Edmunds (roller-skating) Tel (0284) 701215 (bookings), 70216 (management)

SWIMMING

Abbey Pool, Coldham's Common (open-air, heated, summer only)

Bottisham Village College Pool Tel Cambridge 811627 or 811934.

Jesus Green (open-air, summer only)

King's Hedges, North Arbury (bookable learner pool—contact duty officer at Parkside)

Parkside Pool, Mill Road Tel 350008. Indoor pool open daily throughout year. Large pool, learners' pool, spectators' facilities, and cafeteria. Finnish sauna, hot baths and showers also available

Sheep's Green (children's pool, summer only)

Pools also available in a number of other towns in the area.

TENNIS

Major University matches played at Fenner's, Gresham Road. Courts at Jesus Green (hard and grass) and Christ's Pieces (hard)—charges made. Free (hard) courts at Barnwell, Lammas Land and Coleridge and Nightingale Avenue Recreation Grounds.

• • •

Shopping

The main city-centre shops in Cambridge are situated in the area between King's Parade/Trinity Street and Sidney Street/St Andrew's Street, both north and south of Market Street and in the Lion Yard shopping centre. Major chain stores, local department stores and small specialist shops are all well represented. Early closing day is Thursday, but most of the shops are open six days a week.

There is a daily market in Market Square which sells a wide range of goods. Areas tending to have a higher than average concentration of a certain type of shop include Trinity Street for bookshops, Rose Crescent for upmarket clothes and gifts and King's Parade for gift shops. Away from the centre other shopping areas include the new Grafton Centre (to the east of the city centre) and Mill Road.

For advice on consumer affairs contact the Consumer Advice Centre, Central Library *Tel 311318*. Open Mon–Fri 10–1 & 2–4.

EARLY CLOSING DAYS IN SURROUNDING TOWNS

Bedford—Thu
Bury St Edmunds—Thu
Ely—Tue
King's Lynn—Wed
Newmarket—Wed
Peterborough—Mon/Thu
Saffron Walden—Thu
Stowmarket—Tue
Sudbury—Wed
Thaxted—Wed
Thetford—Wed
Wisbech—Wed

ANTIQUE SHOPS IN CAMBRIDGE

In addition to the following shops, the market usually has some stalls selling bric-à-brac and antiques.
Antiques Etcetera, 18 King Street *Tel 62825*
Jess Applin, 8 Lensfield Road *Tel 315168*
John Beazor & Sons Ltd, 78 & 80 Regent Street *Tel 355178*
Buckies, 31 Trinity Street *Tel 357910*
The Cabin, 95a Ditton Walk *Tel 242029*
Malcolm C Clark, 3 Pembroke Street *Tel 357117*
Collectors Market, Dales Brewery, Gwydir Street— antiques and bric-à-brac. Open Mon–Fri 9.30–5, Sat 9.30–5.30
Collins & Clarke, 81 Regent Street *Tel 353801*
Cottage Antiques, 16–18 Lensfield Road *Tel 316698*
Dolphin Antiques, 33 Trumpington Street *Tel 354180*
Gabor Cossa Antiques, 34 Trumpington Street *Tel 356049*
King Street Collections, 56a King Street *Tel 312015*
Lensfield Antiques, 12 Lensfield Road *Tel 357636*
Dorothy Radford, 132 Shelford Road, Trumpington *Tel 840179*
S J Webster–Speakmann, 79 Regent Street *Tel 315048*
Willroy of Dales, Dales Brewery, Gwydir Street *Tel 311687*

BOOKSHOPS

In addition to the bookshops listed below, the market often has stalls selling publishers' remainders and secondhand books, and there are regular bookfairs in the Guildhall and Fisher Hall (details from TIC).
The Bookroom, 13a St Eligius Street *Tel 69694* (antiquarian)
The Bookshop, 24 Magdalene Street *Tel 62417* (secondhand)
Browne's Bookstore, 56 Mill Road *Tel 350968* (new & secondhand)
Cambridge International Book Centre, 42 Hills Road *Tel 65400* (paperbacks, especially English for foreign students)
G R David, 3 & 16 St Edward's Passage *Tel 354619* (remainders, secondhand & antiquarian)
Deighton Bell & Co, 13 Trinity Street *Tel 353939/60791* (antiquarian & secondhand)
Galloway & Porter, 30 Sidney Street *Tel 67876* (new & secondhand); 3 Green Street *Tel 67876* (antiquarian & secondhand)
Grapevine Bookshop, Unit 6, Dales Brewery, Gwydir Street *Tel 61808* (radical progressive literature)
The Green Street Bookshop, 5 Green Street *Tel 68088* (religions, philosophy, history & history of science)
The Haunted Bookshop, St Edward's Passage *Tel 312913* (antiquarian)
W Heffer & Sons, 20 Trinity Street *Tel 358351* (very large stock of new books); 30 Trinity Street *Tel 356200* (children's books); 13 Trinity Street *Tel 61815* (paperbacks); 31 St Andrew's Street *Tel 354778* (paperbacks); 22 The Grafton Centre *Tel 313117* (new incl children's)
A R Mowbray, 14 King's Parade *Tel 358452* (mainly religious)
Quinto, 34 Trinity Street *Tel 358279* (antiquarian & secondhand)
Scripture Union Book Shop, 88a Regent Street *Tel 352727* (religious)
Sherratt & Hughes, 1 Trinity Street *Tel 355488* (new incl academic)
W H Smith & Son, 26 Lion Yard *Tel 311313* (new)

CRAFT SHOPS AND WORKSHOPS IN CAMBRIDGE

All Saints Churchyard, All Saints Passage (off St John's Street), open-air craft market Fri & Sat in Jun, Jul & Aug
Brass Rubbing Centre, St Giles' Church, Castle Street *Tel 61318*. Open Tue–Sat 10–5 & Mon in Jul & Aug
Cambridge Stained Glass, 10 George Street, Willingham *Tel (0954) 60301*
Cobble Yard Craft Centre, Napier Street, off Newmarket Road (various craft workshops)
Fisher Hall Craft Market (nr TIC). Markets every Sat throughout the year, also Fri in Jul and Thu & Fri in Aug. *Tel Ely (0353) 740725* for details

Scotts Bindery, 53 Panton Street *Tel 64862* (bookbinding)

CRAFT SHOPS AND WORKSHOPS OUTSIDE CAMBRIDGE

The shops and workshops listed below are only a selection of those to be found in the area and have been chosen because they are generally open to visitors during normal working hours, though in all cases it is advisable to telephone first to check opening times, exact location and items available.
Abington Pottery, 26 High Street, Little Abington *Tel 891723*
Buckden—L'Bidi Studio, 81 High Street *Tel (0480) 810545*. See under St Ives.
Bury St Edmunds—Barrow Pottery, 27 The Green, Barrow (6m W Bury) *Tel (0284) 810961*
Bury St Edmunds—Clare Craft Pottery, Windy Ridge, Broom Hill Lane, Woolpit (8m E Bury) *Tel Elmswell (0359) 41277*
Bury St Edmunds—Craft at the Suffolk Barn, Fornham Road, Great Barton *Tel Great Barton (028 487) 317* (wide range of crafts for sale—open mid Mar–Dec)
Bury St Edmunds—Elm Tree Cottage Gallery, Gedding Road, Drinkstone Green, nr Bury St Edmunds *Tel Rattlesden (044 93) 366*
Castle Hedingham, The Pottery, 37 St James' Street *Tel Halstead (0787) 60036*
Ely—Steeplegate Ltd, 16–18 High Street *Tel (0353) 4731* (gifts and craft gallery)
Houghton—Alice Green Crafts, Monument House, Thicket Road *Tel Huntingdon (0480) 300977* (flower jewellery and pyrography plus other crafts in shop)
Ickleton—David & Jean Whitaker, Frogge Cottage, 48 Frogge Street *Tel Saffron Walden (0799) 30304* (furniture makers and wood turners)
Mildenhall—Kohl & Son, 2 Finchley Avenue, Industrial Estate *Tel (0638) 712069* (leather goods)
Royston—Foxhall Studio, Kelshall, nr Royston *Tel Kelshall (076 387) 209* (stained-glass windows and other items)
St Ives—John Britton Hand-Engraved Glass, 9 Bridge Street *Tel (0480) 61065*
St Ives—Gem Gardens Glass Art, 18 East Street, Robb's Yard *Tel (0480) 301660*
St Ives—L'Bidi Studio, 40 The Broadway *Tel (0480) 66886* (hand-painted silk goods made and sold together with other craft goods; also gallery displaying work by local artists)
Sawston (6m S Cambridge)— Eastern Counties Sheepskin Tannery Shop *Tel 834757*

Sawston (6m S Cambridge)—
Eastern Counties Sheepskin
Tannery Shop *Tel 834757*
Somersham Pottery, 3 & 4 West
Newlands nr Huntingdon
*Tel Ramsey (Cambs) (0487)
841823* (stoneware, terracotta and
porcelain)
Stilton—Chestnut Country Crafts,
93 North Street *Tel Peterborough
(0733) 240636* or *240016* (shop
selling East Anglian crafts)
Stowmarket—Combs Tannery
Shop (1½m S) *Tel (0449) 674656*
Stowmarket—Museum of East
Anglian Life *Tel (0449) 612229*
(see Places to Visit section for
opening hours)
Thaxted—Glendale Forge, Monk
Street, nr Thaxted *Tel (0371)
830466* (blacksmiths)
Thurston—Mulden End Studio,
Unit 7, Thurston Granary (nr
Bury St Edmunds) *Tel Pakenham
(0359) 32082* (hand-painted
ceramic buildings)
Welney Craft Centre, Croft
House, Main Street, Welney,
Wisbech *Tel Welney (035 471) 238*
(various East Anglian crafts for
sale)
Whittlesey—The Craft Shop/
Whittlesey Miniatures, 6 St

Mary's Street *Tel Peterborough
(0733) 203620* (miniature
figurines and other craft items)

DEPARTMENT STORES

Co-op, Burleigh Street *Tel 358844*
Debenhams, Grafton Centre
Tel 353525
Eaden Lilley, 10 Market Street
Tel 358822
Marks and Spencer, 6 Sidney
Street *Tel 355219*
Robert Sayle, St Andrew's Street
Tel 61292
Joshua Taylor, Sidney Street and
Bridge Street *Tel 314151*
Woolworths, 13 Sidney Street *Tel
357168*

FOOD

Cakes and chocolates:
Fitzbillies, 52 Trumpington Street
Tel 352500. Also at 50 Regent
Street and Eaden Lilley, Market
Street
Delicatessens:
Adams, 13 St John's Street *Tel
350722*; 26 Mill Road *Tel 355013*
Cambridge Continental, 9 The
Broadway, Mill Road *Tel 248069*
Country Gourmet, 84 High Street,
Great Shelford *Tel 845081*
Jason's Shop, 16 Milton Road

Tel 68735
Spencer Stores, 33 Hills Road
Tel 60230
Health/Wholefood shops:
Arjuna, 12 Mill Road *Tel 64845*
Beaumonts Health Store,
Grafton Centre *Tel 314544*
Health Food Store, 3 Rose
Crescent *Tel 353305*
Holland & Barrett, 4 Bradwells
Court *Tel 68914*
Natural Selection Wholefoods,
30 Regent Street *Tel 65819*

NEWSAGENTS

See Useful Information section

PHOTOGRAPHY—
QUICK FILM DEVELOPMENT

See Useful Information section

PRINTS/PICTURES/ART
REPRODUCTIONS

Athena Reproductions Ltd, 19
Lion Yard *Tel 69890*
Benet Gallery, 19 King's Parade
Tel 353783
Cambridge Fine Art, 33 Church
Street, Little Shelford *Tel 842866*
Cambridge Holographics, 29
Magdalene Street *Tel 311322*
Jean Pain, 7 King's Parade
Tel 313970

Transport

AA CENTRES

See Useful Information section

AIR TRAVEL

Cambridge Airport, Newmarket
Road *Tel 61133*. Tours and
charter flights handled by
Premier Airlines Ltd *Tel
Teversham (022 05) 3621*. Air taxi
services operated by Midas Ltd
Tel Teversham (022 05) 3804 and
Cecil Aviation Ltd *Tel 359674*
Stansted Airport (just over ½hr
drive down M11 from
Cambridge). *Tel Bishop's Stortford
(0279) 57641* or *502379*

BICYCLE HIRE

Armada Cycle, 45a Suez Road
Tel 210421
H Drake, 58 Hills Road *Tel 63468*
Geoff's Bike Hire, 65 Devonshire
Road *Tel 65629*
J Hart, 82 Colville Road *Tel 244533*
Ben Hayward & Son, Laundress
Lane *Tel 352294*
Howes Cycles, 104 Regent Street
Tel 350350
W J Ison, 72 Chesterton Road
Tel 315845
N J Thake Cycles, 163–167 Mill
Road *Tel 214999*
University Cycles, 9 Victoria
Avenue *Tel 355517*

BOAT HIRE

The boatyards, situated at Mill
Lane (by Mill Pond) and at

Quayside (near Magdalene Street
Bridge) are open Etr to early Oct.
From Mill Lane punts, rowing
boats and canoes can be taken
either along the Backs or upriver to
Grantchester.
    From Quayside they are available
for the Backs only.
    Punting is not as easy as it
sometimes looks, and visitors may
prefer to hire a chauffeurpunt.
Details available from TIC.

BRITISH RAIL

Station in Station Road to south-
east of city centre.
Passenger enquiries *Tel 311999*
(Mon–Sat 7.30am–9.30pm, Sun
8.30am–9.30pm).
Travel Centre open 5.30am–
10.30pm (Continental Booking 9–
5.30 Mon–Sat).
24hr recorded timetable with
details of main trains to and from
London *Tel 359602*.
Parcel enquiries *Tel 69169*,
Freight services *Tel 358800*.
Trains run approx. hourly to both
Liverpool Street and King's Cross
in London (change at Royston on
the latter service).
British Transport Police
Tel 352031
Stations outside Cambridge:
Bury St Edmunds *Tel (0284) 3947*
Ely (c/o Cambridge *Tel 311999*)
Huntingdon *Tel (0480) 54468*
King's Lynn *Tel (0553) 772021*
Peterborough *Tel (0733) 68181*

BUS AND COACH SERVICES

Cambus Ltd, Cowley Road
Tel 321544.
Inquiry Office at Drummer
Street Bus Station open
Mon–Sat, 8.30–5.30
Tel 355554.
Also hire out 16-seater minibuses
with driver *Tel 69578*
National Express *Tel 460711*
Premier Travel Services,
Drummer Street *Tel 353333*

CAR HIRE

A number of the firms listed below,
indicated (ch), have children's car
seats available. These should
generally be booked in advance.
Avis Rent-A-Car, 243 Mill Road
Tel 212551 (ch)
Budget Rent-A-Car, Newmarket
Road *Tel 323838* (ch)
Tim Brinton Cars Ltd (Peugeot),
147 Hills Road *Tel 213221*
CamKars Hire, 362 Milton Road
Tel 65706
Gilbert Rice Ltd, 350 Newmarket
Road *Tel 315435*
Godfrey Davis Car & Van Hire,
315/345 Mill Road
Tel 248198 (ch)
Hertz (see Willhire)
Kenning Car Hire, 47 Coldham's
Lane *Tel 61538* (ch)
Marshalls Car Hire, Jesus Lane
Tel 62211
Renorent, West's Garage,
Newmarket Road *Tel 351616*

Swan National Car Rental, 264
Newmarket Road *Tel 65438*
F Vindis & Sons, High Street,
Sawston (6m S Cambridge)
Tel 833110 (ch)
Willhire Ltd (Hertz), 41 High
Street, Chesterton *Tel 68888*

CAR PARKING

Mon–Sat (ex BH) between 8.30am
and 6.30pm street parking in
central controlled parking zone
only at metered parking bays.
Short-stay car parks at Lion Yard
(multi-storey), Park Street
(multi-storey), Grafton Centre
(two multi-storey—one entered
from Maid's Causeway, one from
East Road)

Long-stay car parks at Gonville
Place (multi-storey), Saxon
Street and Gold Street
Coach park, City Football
Ground, Milton Road

PETROL—24HR GARAGES

Four Went Ways Self Serve,
Little Abington (7m SW
Cambridge) *Tel Cambridge 835677*

PUNT HIRE

See under Boat hire

RAIL SERVICES

See under British Rail

TAXIS

Taxi ranks at Station (24hr), and

7am–2am at Drummer Street,
Market Hill and St Andrew's St
(by Robert Sayles)

All the following taxi firms are
open at least 7am–7pm.
Those indicated (24hr) are always
open
Al Taxis *Tel 359123* (24hr)
ABC Taxis *Tel 244444* (24hr)
Able Cars *Tel 213232* (24hr)
ACE Taxis *Tel 244469*
Brown's Taxis & Private Hire
Tel 833927
CABCO *Tel 312444*
CAMTAX *Tel 313131* (24hr)
Intercity Taxis *Tel 312233* (24hr)
S & H Taxis *Tel 314314* (24hr)
United Taxis *Tel 352222* (24hr)

—••—

Useful Information

AA

Cambridge—AA 24hr-
breakdown service *Tel 312302*.
Travel shop 46/48 St Andrew's
Street *Tel 66895* (insurance) *65613*
(travel agency)
**Other AA 24hr-breakdown
service nos:**
Bedford *(0234) 218888*
King's Lynn *(0553) 773731*

ADVICE CENTRES

Citizens' Advice Bureau, 2 Pike's
Walk
Tel 356442/353875
Open Mon 9.30–6, Tue–Fri
9.30–4.30, Sat 10–12
Consumer Advice Centre—see
Shopping section

BANKS

All the banks listed are open Mon–
Fri 9.30–3.30.
Barclays and the Midland are
open longer hours and the TSB is
open until 6pm on Friday.
On Saturdays the following
banks are open:
Barclays, Market Hill, 9.30–12;
Midland, Market Hill, 9.30–12.30;
Lloyds, Sidney Street, 10.00–3;
National Westminster, St
Andrew's Street, 9.30–12.30.
Barclays:
15 Bene't Street
92 Cherry Hinton Road
28 Chesterton Road
30 Market Hill
58 Mill Road
76 Newmarket Road
35 Sidney Street
Co-operative Bank:
Burleigh Street
Lloyds:
78 Cherry Hinton Road
Chesterton Road
Lloyds House, Regent Street
90a Mill Road
70 Newmarket Road
95 Regent Street
3 Sidney Street
36 Trinity Street

Midland:
13 Burleigh Street
62 Cherry Hinton Road
58 Chesterton Road
62 Hills Road
32 Market Hill
52 St Andrew's Street
7 The Broadway, Mill Road
National Westminster:
10 Bene't Street
37 Fitzroy Street
56 St Andrew's Street
26 Trinity Street
Royal Bank of Scotland:
28 Trinity Street
Trustee Savings Bank (TSB):
26 Burleigh Street
6 Jesus Lane
224 Mill Road
6 St Andrews Street

BUREAUX DE CHANGE

See also Banks listed above.
Abbott's Travel Agency, 25
Sidney Street *Tel 351636*
**Thomas Cook & Son Travel
Agency,** 5 Market Hill *Tel 66141*

DRY CLEANERS AND
LAUNDERETTES

Dry cleaners:
Sketchley Cleaners, 16 Lion Yard
& 7 Bradwell's Court
Smiths Cleaners, 5a Burleigh
Street and 20 St Andrew's Street
Swiss Laundry Ltd, Cherry
Hinton Road
Launderettes:
1 Arbury Court
115 High Street, Chesterton
28 King Street
161 Mill Road
5 Rectory Terrace, Cherry Hinton
12 Victoria Avenue

EMERGENCY

Fire, Police & Ambulance—dial
999 and tell the Operator which
service you require
Samaritans (24hr service for
suicidal and despairing)—
1 Parker Street
Tel 64455

Services:
Electricity—*Tel 61266* (24hr)
Gas—*Tel 61234* or *Peterborough
(0733) 68911* (office hours),
Freefone 286 or *Potters Bar
(0707) 51234* (after office hours)
Water—Cambridge Water
Company (water supply), Rustat
Road *Tel 247351* (24hr service).
Anglian Water Authority,
Clarendon Road, Cambridge
Tel 61561. Emergency calls
outside office hours. *Tel Stoke
Ferry (0366) 500687*

GUIDED TOURS

A variety of guided tour services
are available from the TIC
(*Tel 322640*) and are summarised
below:
Individual tours—daily walking
tours, generally lasting about 2hrs
and visiting the major colleges (and
where possible King's College
Chapel). Tickets should be
purchased between 24 and ½hr
before the start of the tours which
depart from the TIC at the
following times. Mon–Sat (Apr–
May, 11 & 2, Jun–mid Jun, 11, 1
& 2, mid Jun–Sep, 11, 1, 2 & 3);
Sun (Apr–Sep as weekdays but
11.15 rather than 11); Mon–Sat
(Oct, 11, 1 & 2, Nov, 2); Dec–Mar
Sat (only) 2
Historic Cambridge Tours Jul &
Aug daily at 6.30; also Drama
Tours (details on request)
Group tours—private tours of the
colleges and historical sites, and
tours based on a variety of themes
(e.g. archaeology and
anthropology, education, literature
and libraries, royal Cambridge) can
be arranged.

PLEASE NOTE THAT ANY
GROUP OF TEN OR MORE
PERSONS WISHING TO VISIT
THE COLLEGES MUST BE
ACCOMPANIED BY A BLUE
BADGED CAMBRIDGE
GUIDE

Guided tours also take place in Bury St Edmunds, Ely & King's Lynn. Contact local TIC for details.

HEALTH

Chemists—details of late-night opening are generally listed in the local papers or are available from doctors' surgeries.

Dentists, doctors and opticians are listed in the Yellow Pages telephone directory, and most will provide emergency treatment. If you are unable to find one willing to help contact the Family Practitioner Service *Tel 242731.*

Hospitals (24hr accident and emergency):
Cambridge—Addenbrooke's Hospital, Hills Road *Tel 245151*
Ely—Royal Air Force Hospital, Lynn Road *Tel (0353) 5781*
Huntingdon—Hinchingbrooke Hospital, Hinchingbrooke Park *Tel (0480) 56131*

LIBRARIES & RECORDS OFFICE

Central Library, Lion Yard *Tel 65252.* Lending library and Cambridgeshire Collection (local studies) open Mon–Fri 9.30–6, Sat 9.30–5; reference library open Mon–Fri 9–7, Sat 9–5; exhibition room open Mon–Sat 9–5

Suburban libraries at Arbury Court, Cherry Hinton (High Street), Mill Road, Milton Road (Ascham Road), Newmarket Road and Rock Road

Cambridgeshire Records Office, Shire Hall *Tel 317281.* Open Mon–Fri 9–12.45, 1.45–5.15 (or 4.15 Fri) and by appt Tue 5.15–9pm

NEWSAGENTS

Adams & Dellar, 77 Regent Street
Bridge, 18 Magdalene Street
Burleigh Newsagents, 42 Burleigh Street
Castle Street Newsagents, 4 Castle Street
City Newspapers, 8 Market Passage
The Corner Shop, 251 Chesterton Road
Douglas & Wilson, 301 Mill Road
Forbuoys, 1 Adkins Corner, Perne Road, 41 Arbury Court & 132 Wulfstan Way
Grey Davis News, 41 Trumpington Street
Kings Newsagents, 214 Mill Road
Lambert & Ward, 46 Hills Road
Lavells Ltd, 72 Mill Road
NSS Newsagents, 108 Cherry Hinton Road & 11 Victoria Avenue
Newnham Newsagents, 38 Newnham Road
Nicholsons Whites News, 115 Perne Road
M & S Orbell, 22 Victoria Road
Rossendale, The Kiosk, Fitzroy Street
W H Smith, 26 Lion Yard, &

Railway Station
Stops Shops Newsagents, 84 Campkin Road, 239 Cherry Hinton Road, 158 Hills Road, 279 Newmarket Road
Uff, 109 Milton Road
United News, 18 Bradwell's Court
Vinery News, 1 Vinery Way
Whites News, 12 King's Parade

NEWSPAPERS

Cambridge Evening News & Cambridge Weekly News, 51 Newmarket Road *Tel 358877*
Town Crier, Unit 1, The Techno Park, Newmarket Road *Tel 69966*

PHOTOGRAPHY—QUICK FILM DEVELOPMENT

AM Photographic, 31 Clifton Road *Tel 213271* (2–3hr)
Anglia Photoworks, 66 Devonshire Road *Tel 355998* (film in by 10.30am, ready by 5pm)
The Cambridge Photographers, 4 Hills Road *Tel 62857* (approx 24hr service)
Colourquick Ltd, 58 Regent Street *Tel 69291* (film in by 9am, ready midday; in after midday, ready next day)
Photolab Express, c/o Boots the Chemist, 28 Petty Cury *Tel 68580* (1hr & 24hr service)
United Photofinishers Ltd, 36 Humberstone Road *Tel 65651* (film in by 4pm, ready next day at 10am)

POLICE STATIONS

Cambridge—Parkside *Tel 358966*
Ely—Nutholt Lane *Tel (0353) 2392*
Huntingdon—Ferrars Road *Tel (0480) 56111*

POST OFFICES

Main Post Office 9–11 St Andrew's Street *Tel 351212.* Open Mon–Fri 9–5.30, Sat 9–1. Last collection Mon–Fri 7.45. Also 23–24 Trinity Street and elsewhere in suburbs of city
Sorting Office, Mill Road. Last collection Mon–Fri 7.30, Sat 1

RADIO (LOCAL STATIONS)

Hereward Radio *Tel Peterborough (0733) 46225.* Broadcast on 1332 kHz (225m), VHF 102.7MHz
Radio Cambridgeshire *Tel 315970.* Broadcast (South Cambs) on 1449kHz (207m), VHF 103.9MHz and (North Cambs) on 1026kHz (292m), VHF 96MHz
Radio Saxon *Tel Bury St Edmunds (0284) 701511.* Broadcast on 1251kHz (240m), VHF 96.4MHz

TOILETS

Those indicated (d) are accessible to those in wheelchairs
Alexandra Gardens (off Carlyle Road)
Chesterton Road (d)
Drummer Street (d)

Grafton Centre
Jesus Green (nr footbridge to Chesterton Road)
Lion Yard (d)—near library
Newnham Road (Lammas Land)
Northampton Street
Park Street Car Park (d)
Parker's Piece (Gonville Place)
Quayside (d)

TOURIST INFORMATION CENTRES

Cambridge—Wheeler Street *Tel 322640.* Open all year Mon–Fri 9–5.30 (9–6 Mar–Oct, Jul & Aug 9–7), Sat 9–5; May–Sep Sun & BH (10.30–3.30). Closed Good Fri, Chr & New Year
Bury St Edmunds—Abbey Gardens, Angel Hill *Tel (0284) 64667.* Open early May–Sep Mon–Fri 9–5.30, Sat 10–4.30; Jul & Aug only Sun 10–12. During winter months Thingoe House, Northgate Street *Tel (0284) 63233 ext 427* (Mon–Thu 9–5.20, Fri 9–4.25)
Ely—The Library, Palace Green *Tel (0353) 2062.* Open Mon (10–7), Tue (10–5), Wed, Thu (10–6), Fri (10–7), Sat (9.30–5); & Sun & BH 12–4 (Jun–Sep)
Huntingdon—The Library, Princes Street *Tel (0480) 425831.* Open Oct–Mar Mon–Fri 10–6, Sat 9–5; Apr–Sep Mon–Fri 9.30–5.30, Sat 9–5.
King's Lynn—The Old Goal House, Saturday Market Place *Tel (0553) 763044.* Open all year Mon–Fri 10–5 (or 4.30 Fri); also May–Oct Sat 10–4
Lavenham—The Guildhall, Market Place *Tel (0787) 248207.* Open Apr–Sep daily 10–5
Peterborough—Town Hall, Bridge Street *Tel (0733) 63141.* Mon–Fri 9–5; Jun–Aug Sat 10–1. Also Central Library, Broadway *Tel (0733) 48343 ext 36.* Mon–Fri 10–7 (5pm Thu), Sat 9.30–5. Closed BH Mon & Tue
Saffron Walden—Corn Exchange, Market Square *Tel (0799) 24282.* Open all year (ex BH) Mon–Sat 9.30–4.30 (Nov–Mar 10–4)
Sudbury—Public Library, Market Hill *Tel (0787) 72092.* Open Tue, Thu & Sat 9.30–5, Wed 9.30–1, Fri 9.30–7.30
Thetford—Ancient House Museum, White Hart Street *Tel (0842) 2599.* Open all year (ex Good Fri & 25–26 Dec), Mon 10–1 & 2–5, Tue–Sat 10–5; also Sun 2–5 (late May–late Sep only)
Wisbech—District Library, Ely Place *Tel (0945) 583263.* Tue & Wed 10–6, Thu & Fri 10–7, Sat 9.30–5. Tel enquiries only 9–5

View from Magdalene Street Bridge. Punts can be hired near by

Main entries are shown in **bold**

Acknowledgements

MALC BIRKITT WAS ESPECIALLY COMMISSIONED BY THE AUTOMOBILE ASSOCIATION FOR THIS PUBLICATION. ALL THE PHOTOGRAPHS EXCEPT THOSE LISTED BELOW WERE TAKEN BY HIM.

M ADELMAN *76 Finchingfield;* BRITAIN ON VIEW *Cover King's College Chapel;* CAMBRIDGE AERIAL PHOTOGRAPHY *16 Aerial View of Cambridge;* THE CAMBRIDGESHIRE COLLECTION *8 Rowing coach, May races; 9 Pot Fair; 11 Bucket dredger, Gang dredging, 12 Old Fen, Paul & Sally Gotobed, 13 Papyruseun, Stourbridge Fair; 16 Bull Hotel, 18 Rugger Man, Installation ceremony, 19 William Gretton, Professor Willis; 20 King's College Chapel, 119 Peterhouse;* CAMBRIDGE COUNTY RECORD OFFICE *14/15 North West Prospect; 26 Parker's Piece dinner;* CAMBRIDGE NEWSPAPERS *9 Madgrigals, Midsummer Fair;* FITZWILLIAM MUSEUM *38 Entrance hall, Harlequin, 39 Feather fan, Le Printemps;* FRANCIS FRITH COLLECTION *15 Cambridge 1909;* JARROLD COLOUR LIBRARY *21 King's College Chapel choir;* THE MANSELL COLLECTION *28 Robert Devereux, Oliver Cromwell, Nicholes Ridley, 29 Samuel Pepys, William Pitt, William Wordsworth; 30 Lord Byron, Alfred Tennyson; 31 Charles Darwin, Ernest Rutherford, 32 Rupert Brooke;* MARY EVANS PICTURE LIBRARY *17 Peterhouse, 19 Undergraduates room;* S & O MATHEWS *69 Royston Caves, 75 Vineyard, 76/7 Hatfield Forest, 77 Ickworth House, 79 Guildhall, 81 Melford Hall, 87 Thetford Priory, 95 Bourn Windmill;* THE NATIONAL TRUST PHOTOGRAPHIC LIBRARY *93 Anglesey Abbey;* REX FEATURES *32 Prince Edward;* R SURMAN *4/5 King's Back, 5 Market; 72 Angel Hill, 79 Guildhall;* H WILLIAMS *87 Thetford Forest, 89 Wimpole Hall*